Empirical Modeling in Economics

In these three essays, Professor Granger explains the process of constructing and evaluating an empirical model. Drawing on a wide range of cases and vignettes from economics, finance, politics, and environment economics, as well as from art, literature, and the entertainment industry, Professor Granger combines rigor with intuition to provide a unique and entertaining insight into one of the most important subjects in modern economics.

Chapter 1 deals with Specification. The process of specifying a model is discussed using deforestation in the Amazon region of Brazil as an illustration. Chapter 2 considers Evaluation, and argues that insufficient evaluation is undertaken by economists, and that models should be evaluated in terms of the quality of their output. In chapter 3, the question of how to evaluate forecasts is considered at several levels of increasing depth and using a more sophisticated, technical approach than in the earlier two chapters.

CLIVE W.J. GRANGER is widely regarded as one of the most important figures in the development of econometrics. He currently holds the Chancellor's Associates Chair in Economics at the University of California, San Diego. He was elected a fellow at the American Academy of Arts and Sciences in 1995.

Empirical Modeling in Economics

Specification and Evaluation

———✢———

Clive W.J. Granger

Professor of Economics
University of California, San Diego

CAMBRIDGE
UNIVERSITY PRESS

HB
141
.G73
1999

PUBLISHED BY THE PRESS SYNDICATE OF THE UNIVERSITY OF CAMBRIDGE
The Pitt Building, Trumpington Street, Cambridge, United Kingdom

CAMBRIDGE UNIVERSITY PRESS
The Edinburgh Building, Cambridge, CB2 2RU, UK http://www.cup.cam.ac.uk
40 West 20th Street, New York, NY 10011-4211, USA http://www.cup.org
10 Stamford Road, Oakleigh, Melbourne 3166, Australia

First published 1999

Printed in the United Kingdom at the University Press, Cambridge

Typeset in 10.5/16pt Meridien in QuarkXPress® [SE]

A catalogue record for this book is available from the British Library

ISBN 0 521 66208 7 hardback
ISBN 0 521 77825 5 paperback

Contents

Foreword

It is a privilege and a pleasure to write a foreword to the published version of Clive Granger's 1998 Marshall Lectures which I much enjoyed listening to. Granger has made fundamental contributions to modern econometrics, both to its conceptual underpinnings and to its techniques. In the lectures he brought to bear wisdom accumulated during 40 years of teaching and research to discuss the conceptual difficulties associated with empirical work in economics. He has always argued that the bridge between economic theory and applied economics should be a sturdy structure, across which it was both necessary and safe for practitioners to go in both directions. He is also one of those, unhappily all too rare, highly imaginative and creative persons who are never afraid to ask (seemingly) simple questions, nor to give simple answers. He is undogmatic and open-minded, with as firm a grasp on fundamental economic principles as on approaches to and techniques in econometrics, not a few of which are his inventions. To cap it all, he is splendid company, as much at home in a coffee room or nattering with students as at a formal dinner with the great and the good.

In the first chapter Granger discusses the practical optimum way of analyzing the economic and social impact of deforestation in the Brazilian portion of the Amazon rain forest. He sets out the pros and cons and the incoherencies in the measurement of the variables to be used, the measurement of which is derived from a large data set of differing quality. His discussion of what the raw measures may mean is an object lesson for anyone who wishes to critically approach and use a data set. The same may be said of how he teases out from the context the appropriate models to be used – what **exactly** is supplied and demanded, for example.

In the second chapter, on the evaluation of empirical models, Granger bases his wide-ranging discussion mainly on two examples, Robert Hall's random walk theory of consumption expenditure and Daniel Suits's estimation of the elasticity of demand for watermelons. He is concerned with the crucial issue, how do we evaluate evaluations? His own philosophy is clearly stated – most economic research should not be considered to be like pure mathematics (at which, nevertheless, Granger himself is quite a dab hand) but should be associated with clear-cut and precisely stated objectives. His principle conclusion is that evaluation should be related to the quality of the *output* of research, using economic measures – down-to-earth, sensible, and relevant. In the chapter, as well as showing command over what he is writing about, he also provides examples which take in the writings of current Cambridge teachers together with those of Alfred Marshall and Maynard Keynes. He also mentions Marshall's Uncle Charles in Australia who lent Alfred the funds which allowed him to become an economist (by reading for the mathematics tripos at St John's). In a footnote Granger says that just before he gave the lecture, he was told that the background to the loan was not as graphic, nor was Uncle Charles as altruistic, as Keynes originally had him. I must confess to being the party-pooper responsible for telling Clive this.

Chapter 3 (which is additional to the original lectures) is more technical. It is concerned with developments on the frontier of modern econometrics. Granger has considerately divided the chapter into sections, with general explanations of issues and tasks preceding the accounts of specific technical research. The same basic philosophy underlies the discussions and the results reported – that models should be useful to decision makers so that we must always evaluate the quality of the outputs of models and not merely the apparent quality of the models themselves. Most of the examples concern forecasting of one sort or another and constitute a plea for other workers to take on board, if they have not done so already, the ideas and developments reported here. As Granger says, much of the discussion is highly technical but it is relieved by a dry wit and gems of common sense, for example, that cost functions used to evaluate different methods may be asymmetric. Thus, the costs of being 10 minutes early for a flight (or a lecture) are quite different from those of being 10 minutes late.

May I recommend the chapters that follow for their wisdom, common sense and relevance? An added bonus is that they may also serve to introduce those readers who have not met Clive, or heard him in person, to one of the most engaging and likeable characters in our trade.

G.C. HARCOURT
February 1999

— ✝ x ✝ —

Acknowledgments

I would like to thank the faculty of the Department of Economics and the University of Cambridge for doing me the honor of inviting me to give the Alfred Marshall Lectures in 1998. I would particularly like to thank Professor Bill Brown, who was Chair at the time of the invitation, Professor Partha Dasgupta, who was Chair when I gave the lectures and hosted my visit to the Department, and to Professor M. Hashem Pesaran and Dr. Amarta Sen, Master-of-Trinity, who arranged and allowed me the comfort of staying at Trinity College. I would particularly like to thank Dr. Geoff Harcourt for making me, and many other visitors, feel so welcome in the Department and for writing an introdution about the lectures.

The Marshall Lectures themselves discuss, at a level suitable for senior undergraduates at Cambridge, how an empirical economist approaches the task of constructing a model and then how such models can be evaluated. As an example, I have used results obtained by a group, including myself, who considered the dynamics of the deforestation process in the Amazon region of Brazil. This was a one year National Science Foundation funded project involving Lykke Andersen, Lily Huang, Eustaquio Reis, and Diana Weinhold, which achieved a lot. It was unfortunate that we could not get a second year of funding.

To the Marshall Lectures I have added a further essay on the evaluation of forecasts using a more sophisticated level of mathematical argument. I have taken this opportunity of putting into context several pieces of research with which I have been involved in the last few months, including work with Dr. Mark Machina and Professor M. Hashem Pesaran.

Finally I would like to thank Michael J. Bacci for undertaking the task of preparing the manuscripts with a continuously positive approach.

I hope that the ideas presented will influence others to think further on these and related topics.

CLIVE W.J. GRANGER
December 1998

CHAPTER ONE

The specification of empirical models

Models and changes

On May 25, 1961 President John F. Kennedy issued a challenge to the scientists and engineers of the United States to put an American on the moon by the end of the decade. The first moon landing took place on July 20, 1969. To meet the challenge many research problems had to be solved in rocketry, control theory, materials science, and in other fields. This was successfully completed in the appropriate sequence, within the dead-line and, I believe, within the cost constraints imposed by Congress. This is an example of a successful challenge. It had substantial funding attached and the researchers embraced it with some enthusiasm, clearly believing that the objective was achievable. In contrast, on May 18, 1997, President William J. Clinton challenged the US health community to find a vaccine to prevent AIDS within the next decade but he did not promise extra funding. The response was muted, some saying that the challenge was impossible, some that it would be better to try to find a cure for AIDS rather than a preventative vaccine and there has been little discussion of this challenge since.

How would economists respond to a similar challenge? Economists in a country could be asked to attempt to solve, or at least reduce, some particular economic problem. Possible examples of such problems would be if there were small regions that had clearly lower income levels or growth rates or if some groups in the economy faced particularly high unemployment rates. The challenge to the economists would be to alleviate these perceived difficulties within a given horizon and for an agreed cost. A different challenge might be to consider how to make efficient use of senior citizens, aged say 60 to 75, who are mentally active, are less able physically, but who do not wish to fully retire. In another example, economists could be asked to find economic incentives supplied by the richer countries to persuade Brazil to reduce deforestation in its rain forests. Given some funding, could the economists in the nation(s) organize themselves to tackle the problem, specify what the problem is in a precise form and state what would comprise a solution that would be satisfactory to the challenger? I have been talking to colleagues about this possibility and they are not optimistic. A common position is that if the economists ever did find a solution it would not be acceptable to other major policy-making groups in society with their own viewpoints, such as politicians, lawyers, sociologists, and journalists, and so the economist's solution would not be accepted by society unless it was a Pareto optimum. However this viewpoint can be ameliorated by using second-best solutions and large doses of bargaining and game theory which economists should be good at.

Some possible challenges are difficult to define. Suppose that the economists are asked to substantially reduce poverty but that the government statisticians define poverty as those falling into the lowest 12 percent of the income distribution. In this case poverty can never be solved as there will always be 12 percent at the bottom of whatever income distribution occurs. An alternative definition of poverty may be arbitrary in some other way.

There have been two minor challenges to economists in recent years of which I am aware. In the EC econometricians have been encouraged to study whether there is evidence for convergence of regional economies towards some aggregate level. The question is obviously of interest to politicians in a community of countries about to adopt a common currency. The difficulty with this research has been in deciding on the correct definition of convergence. A number of definitions have been used, some of which are quite unsatisfactory. In the US economists have been provided with extra funds to study the economics of global warming. For several years Congress has provided these funds to the National Science Foundation which were then allocated using competitive bids. Unfortunately there was no clear objective for the research and so it has been dissipated over many topics rather than being focused in just a few directions. However, the main example that I will be using in this lecture is based on a global warming project. Overall, I think that economists and their techniques when evaluated and compared to results from other fields have performed in a bimodal way; sometimes rather well, sometimes badly. This may be because the challenges are so poorly defined.

To tackle a practical problem an economist will need to build an empirical model. That is, a model of the actual economy or at least that part of it that is relevant to the problem. The main topic covered in this chapter is the process of building such a model. That is, its specification, interpretation, cost, what it is not, and how it varies according to its objectives. In my second chapter I will discuss the important questions concerning the evaluation of models: How do we know if a model is any good and how that will depend on the objective of the modeling exercise.

A relevant starting point is to admit that there is no single clearly best way of approaching the question of how to specify an empirical model. Virtually every econometrician and applied economist has their own way and we can each point out weaknesses in the approach used by others. The result is that several different models are produced rather than just one and I view this as a strength in the situation rather than a weakness as it means that we have different models to compare and then we learn by making comparisons. As new data arrive it is easier to hill-climb to better models using several starting points than just a single one.

Eventually it will be necessary to concentrate on just a few of the models and drop the rest, but this is best done after a proper evaluation exercise, preferably using a post or out of sample data set.

There are several reasons for the lack of agreement between empirical modelers but a major one is the huge complexity of a modern economy. In the US, for example, the population of over 260 million contains about 100 million family units all making many economic decisions hourly, daily, weekly, monthly, annually, or longer depending on the type of decision. Only a very small percentage of the economic outcomes from these decisions are recorded, such as purchases, hours worked, and investments made. Of these only an extremely small percentage are made public. Government and some private agencies collect these data, aggregate them, possibly seasonally adjust them, and then make them generally available. Even with standard data sets there is too much information to use in the typical model. It is thus necessary to begin by selecting variables to be used and finding the corresponding available data, perhaps after using both temporal and cross-sectional aggregation. All this implies that the eventual model will certainly be an approximation to the actual economy, but probably a very crude approximation. Because of this inevitable reduction process, from the many decisions that make up the actual economy to the empirical model, and the many possible ways to form an approximation, it is obvious why various alternative models can occur. Clearly at some point in the modeling process some selection process will have to be applied, as part of the evaluation procedure.

Before proceeding I need to make clear a piece of terminology. In what follows I will restrict the use of the word "model" just to empirical models based on data from an actual economy. Such models will often be distinguished from information in the form of what may be called theory. In this simplistic viewpoint a theory starts with a set of consistent assumptions and then produces logical consequences from them in a form relevant to economic questions. On some occasions this theory is best expressed using very sophisticated mathematics, "best" here meaning the most rigorous and compact although not necessarily the easiest to understand. To have something easier to use and to interpret a simple version of the theory can be formed, an approximation, and this is sometimes called a theoretical model. However, I will call all such constructs just "theory." I will take the attitude that a piece of theory has only intellectual interest until it has been validated in some way against alternative theories and using actual data.

A sculptor once said that the way he viewed his art was that he took a large block of stone and just chipped it away until he revealed the sculpture that was hidden inside it. Some empirical modelers view their task in a similar fashion starting with a mass of data and slowly discarding them to get at a correct representation. My perception is quite different. I think of a modeler as starting with some disparate pieces – some wood, a few bricks, some nails, and so forth – and attempting to build an object for which he (or she) has only a very inadequate plan, or theory. The modeler can look at related constructs and can use institutional information and will eventually arrive at an approximation of the object that they are trying to represent, perhaps after several attempts. Model building will be a team effort with inputs from theorists, econometricians, local statisticians familiar with the data, and economists aware of local facts or relevant institutional constraints. As projects get large, the importance of team-work becomes emphasized.

The Amazon project

I will illustrate many of the problems faced when undertaking an empirical study by using parts of a study of the dynamics of deforestation in the Amazon region of Brazil. The analysis attempted to consider how the rate of change of deforestation is influenced by economic, demographic, and policy changes.

It is useful to start with some basic facts. The Amazon rain forest is the largest remaining uncleared forest in the world covering about 5.5 million square kilometers or 2.12 million square miles. Sixty percent of this forest lies in Brazil and so this section covers about 3.55 million square kilometers or 1.37 million square miles. Such numbers are difficult to appreciate so perhaps it is more useful to say that the rain forest in Brazil is about the same size as the UK plus France, Germany, Finland, Norway, Sweden, Denmark,

Italy, Spain, Portugal, Greece, Belgium, The Netherlands, Austria and Ireland. That is, all of the EC countries plus Norway. It is perhaps interesting to note that most of these countries were heavily forested 1000 years ago. Deforestation there resulted in excellent agricultural land which eventually supported the Industrial Revolution and still remains productive.

To study such a region one requires some data. Fortunately Estaquio Reis, an economist working in Rio de Janeiro, had gathered a panel data set, based on over 300 sub-regions or municipalities for four time periods five years apart. Values for well over a hundred variables had been obtained for each region and year, giving about two hundred thousand individual items of data or numbers. The variables included summaries of local employment, income, agricultural production and prices, population level and change, forestry output and prices, mining production for various materials and metals, and land use estimates for various categories. For example the land use could be divided into original forest, regrown forest, fallow land which may include wet-land, land used for growing crops, and, finally, land used for grazing animals. Once land is used for agriculture it depreciates and one land use naturally converts into another, as will be analyzed later.

Many of the variables being discussed are difficult to define and therefore particularly difficult to measure. Consider whether or not a particular piece of land should be classified as "forested." It may well contain a number of groups of trees with shrubs in between but exactly what quantity and configuration of trees constitutes a forest? Even if each local statistician has a sensible and consistent way of making a decision, remember that in each of the over three hundred municipalities a different person is measuring many of the critical variables and also that very likely different people will be involved when the next set of measurements are taken five years later. The quality of the data is likely to be quite low when different people are making measurements on quantities that are difficult to define and often over very large regions for which travel is difficult and resources available for data collection are limited. The municipalities vary greatly in size; a few are larger than the UK but many are smaller than a typical old-fashioned county. This produces another potential problem in that if there is a serious mis-recording of some number, then a statistician sitting in Brasilia compiling the data from all the regions may not recognize the error because he or she may not have very strong priors about what to expect. This would not be true of interest rates, for example. If most regions were reporting rates around 8 percent but one region reported 80 percent it would clearly be a reporting error. However values for the area that had been deforested in the last five years would be less easy to interpret. Although most of the data we used in our study appeared to be of good quality there was also plenty of evidence that not all of the two hundred thousand pieces of data were perfect. The reaction is that so-called robust methods of analysis have to be used and then interpretation of the results conducted with some care.

The ground-based measures of land use, and thus of deforestation, can be compared to measures obtained from satellite imaging. One of the benefits of the Cold War was the development of very high quality satellite spy photography. Satellites will occasionally pass over the region and accurate photos taken which are then interpreted and a measure of the amount of forest remaining in a region can be obtained. Potentially this is an accurate measure but, being a rain forest, often large regions are obscured by clouds. The ground and space measurements usually agree quite closely but not on all occasions. An example is when a forest edges up to fallow land, the edge consisting of small thin trees perhaps over a wide range. The two methods of measurement are inclined to place the edge of the forest at different places. It was found that the values from space are often helpful for checking the ground-based estimates.

When starting to build a model it is certainly useful to begin with a theoretical foundation but it is important that the theory be relevant. For deforestation an obvious starting point, it would seem, would be consideration of supply and demand. The supply side is fairly easy; it is fixed in the short and medium term as the standing timber and this can be measured, but with some difficulty and thus error. However, the demand side requires a little more thought. The reason for there being a demand for wood varies around the world, apart from the special hard woods used for expensive furniture which are becoming difficult to find everywhere. In parts of Africa and Southeast Asia wood is largely used as a fuel, for heating and cooking, whereas in the more developed countries the major uses are for construction, furniture and paper. Taking either viewpoint it would be quite easy to specify a demand equation using explanatory variables such as timber prices, population size, income levels, and so forth. Although sensible, such an equation would be quite inappropriate for the Amazon region of Brazil where deforestation occurs not because of demand for wood but due to demand for the land on which the trees stand. Poor farmers cut down the forest, burn it, clear the land, and use it to grow crops. This oversimplified account suggests that the correct starting point is the use of supply and demand but applied to cleared land rather than to wood. A demand equation for this land would perhaps concentrate on new farmers in the region, such as immigrants, but again the actual process being studied is rather more complicated. The newly cleared land that is being planted with crops is of poor quality and deteriorates rather quickly until it can no longer be used economically for growing crops but can be used for grazing cattle and sheep. Sometimes the land deteriorates even further and becomes fallow and is possibly of little agricultural value. This discarded land may become forest again over a very long period but over the time span considered by the data this possibility is not relevant. The transition from long-term forest through deforestation to crop land, pasture, and on to long-term fallow land is quite different to

Table 1.1

	NEWCLEAR$_t$	CRP$_{t-1}$	PAS$_{t-1}$	FAL$_{t-1}$
CRP$_t$	0.10	0.66	0	0.08
PAS$_t$	0.30	0	1.0	0.11
FAL$_t$	0.60	0.34	0	0.81

that experienced in Northern Europe or in North America where forests were cut down centuries ago to reveal rich land that has been used successfully ever since, with careful husbandry, and mostly for crops.

For a typical piece of land one has the transition matrix shown in table 1.1. There are three land uses shown: CRP is crop, PAS is pasture, FAL is fallow and NEWCLEAR is land that has been cleared from forest since the previous survey five year ago. The values shown are all essentially transition probabilities and so are quantities between 0 and 1. Thus if for a region CRP$_{t-1}$ | FAL$_t$ is 0.34 it means that 34 percent of the ex-crop land is fallow. NEWCLEAR is the land at time t that did not exist at time $t-1$. Fallow occasionally is included in agricultural land as some of it may have use, either directly or is being held out for later use. The values shown in the table are rather idealized for ease of presentation. It will be seen that they add to one down the columns as each piece of land in some category at time $t-1$ has to be re-allocated at time t. If we take the figures at their face value there seems to be two types of land: that which is suitable for pasture and that which is used for crops.

Old pasture land becomes current pasture land, which is supplemented by 30 percent of the newly cleared land. Thus land classified as pasture will be increasing in quantity, although not necessarily in quality, and much of the land produced by deforestation, within five years, has become pasture, possibly having briefly passed through a crops use stage. Thirty four percent of the old crop land is lost to the fallow category within the five year span, the remaining 66 percent staying as crop land. Current crop land is made up of new cleared land, old crop land, and some old fallow land. Current fallow land includes 60 percent of the land that was newly cleared by deforestation over the last five years, a remarkably large percentage, plus 34 percent of the old crop land but it largely consists of previous fallow land. The amount of fallow land is obviously increasing.

The speed with which newly cleared land becomes pasture, and particularly fallow land over just a five year period and the relatively small contribution it makes to enhancing the stock of crop land suggests that clearing the forest is not an efficient use of the resource. One criticism is that much of the deforestation is done by the cattle indus-try. The increase in pasture supports this. The figures given in the table are not exact and will vary somewhat by using different estimation methods and different sub-regions of Amazonia but the message remains the same. For the farmers and peasants already in the region to continue crop production at current levels extensive deforestation is needed. Thus deforestation will occur without any new immigrants due just to soil depreciation and current methods of land use. The transition matrix in table 1.1 can only be produced from a panel survey of many districts over several time periods, its formulation and estimation involves little economics but the values obtained suggest relevant economic questions to ask and possible specifications for explanatory models. The initial objective is to quantify the deforestation process and the long-term implications of allowing this process to continue. It may then be possible to consider policies that would slow the destruction of trees in this rain forest, which is considered to be a world resource of considerable value. One such policy would be to somehow boost non-farm employment in the region whilst at the same time importing cheap crops and food. It would certainly be possible to model agricultural production in a typical region and to measure the reaction of farmers to changes in food prices and policies. However, to examine the long-run implications for deforestation it is most appropriate to directly form a demand equation for newly cleared land.

If the variable to be modeled is NEWCLEAR there are many possible explanatory variables that can be considered including various local population measures, previous clearing values, clearing levels in neighboring regions, income per capital, road length, river length, distance to federal and state capitals, area of municipality, and policy variables. The Brazilian government in some periods and locations was encouraging agricultural settlement, largely by designating certain regions as "growth poles" which enjoyed extra favorable investment and tax conditions and by issuing credit incentives granted by the Superintendency for Amazon Development (SUDAM) to some regions. It would be quite easy to write down a sensible model specification, estimate the coefficients by any of several available techniques and then to present the results for interpretation. There are, however, a number of possible pitfalls and problems with such a seemingly simple approach. Some of these are discussed in the following sections.

Model building

For the moment I want to step away from the deforestation study and discuss some of the general questions that arise when building an empirical model. It is useful to propose the existence of a data-generating mechanism to explain the fact that new data are generated almost continuously. As explained earlier, the true mechanism will be extremely complicated and its information will be transformed in many ways from the outcomes of decisions made by economic agents to the data that eventually appear out of the system. One has to hope that these data capture the essential features of the economy and that an empirical model will provide a useful approximation to the generating mechanism of these data.

The classical approach to constructing a model starts with a sound, internally consistent, economic theory which provides a tight specification for the empirical model. This model is then estimated and interpreted. Unfortunately, this strategy towards modeling has not always proved to be a successful one. Models produced in this way often do not fit the data in various important directions. As one pair of applied economists put it, "a recurring problem in empirical studies of consumer and producer behavior is that the regularity properties implied by microeconomic theory have more often than not been rejected" (Rezili and Ozanne (1997)), who then go on to say "such rejection means that empirical work loses a good deal of its theoretical credibility." They point out that a major problem is "the failure of static equilibrium theory to account for dynamic aspects of consumer and producer behavior" and show how the introduction of dynamics into an equilibrium model, by use of a structure known as an error-correcting model, leads to clear improvements. In macroeconomics there has often been a problem relating a theory with the dynamics that might be associated with disequilibrium. The theory often fails to capture vital features of the data, such as trends or seasonal components or some of the structural breaks.

The question of how to use economic theory when constructing an empirical model has generated considerable controversy. One can find advocates at both extremes, some saying that theory contains the only pure truth and so has to be the basis of the model, even to claiming that all "residuals" have to have theoretical explanations, leaving little place for stochastics, uncertainty, or exogenous shocks to the system. At the other extreme, some econometricians have thrown up their hands in despair when trying to find a use for theory and so build "atheoretical" models based just on examination of the data and using any apparent regularities and relationships found in it. Most applied economists take a middle ground, using theory to provide an initial specification and then data exploration techniques to extend or refine the starting model, leading to a form that better represents the data. A formal way to link economic theory and empirical econometrics has been the central aim of a research program by a Norwegian economist, Bernt Stigum, discussed in a lengthy book (1990) and several subsequent papers (e.g. 1995). He discusses how most economic theory is unsuitable for direct empirical use and in what manner the theorist and the econometrician should collaborate to produce a "bridge" from the pristine theory to the more pragmatic data analysis. As a simple example, a theory may relate a variable at time t to another variable at time $t-1$, without any indication of the physical length of the time interval involved: is it a minute, a day, a week, or a month? The answer to this question is very important to the econometrician translating the theory into a practical model.

It is generally accepted that basing a model on a correct theory is good practice, but how do we know if a theory is correct? That is partly my topic for chapter 2. If there are several competing theories they will lead to alternative models which is anathema to anyone taking a scientific viewpoint. However, if we consider economic modelers as producers of commodities and the users of the models as consumers, it is worth remembering that consumers usually prefer having a choice. It is rare for one model to be superior for all possible purposes: forecasting, policy making, conditional forecasts, testing hypotheses, or investigating the effects of a previous policy change, for example. Different users will have different tastes, beliefs, and needs, and will prefer certain types of models. Clearly model providers will not only have to produce the models but also relevant summary statistics allowing model consumers to make sensible choices between them. It is not enough to declare "my model is good" but you should also be expected to prove it!

If no theoretical basis is used and if a complex modeling situation is considered, with many possible explanatory variables and plenty of data, the possibility of "data-mining" or "data-snooping" becomes a problem, particularly now that computing is both fast and cheap. Clearly evaluation procedures need to be applied using data sets that were not involved in the model selection and estimation process, either "out-of-sample" in cross-section or panel analysis, or "post-sample" in time series. It is not sufficient to merely show a statistic that indicates that one model performs better than others; a correct hypothesis test is required, but this takes us into rather technical areas.

One of the basic properties of a model is that it should "balance," in fact every equation in a system should balance.

To illustrate this idea, consider a single, linear equation with two explanatory variables

$$Y_t = a + b_1 X_{1t} + b_2 X_{2t} + e_t.$$

Suppose from looking at plots of the variables, or by "pre-testing," it is found that some contain a dominating statistical property but that others do not, then these properties have to balance on the two sides of the equation. It is assumed that e_t does not contain the property. Thus, for example, if Y_t contains a clear trend but neither X variable does, the explanatory part of the model cannot explain an important component of the dependent variable Y; and so the equation will be unbalanced. If Y_t and X_{2t} had no trends but X_{1t} had a trend, the equation would balance only if $b_1 = 0$, so now the property determines part of the specification. The same comments would apply if the dominant property was a strong seasonal or a unit root, sometimes called a long-memory or persistence property because the effect of a shock on the economy is noticeable for a long time. The balance question becomes a little more subtle if Y_t does not have the dominant property but both X_{1t}, X_{2t} do have it. It is possible, although somewhat unlikely, that a linear combination of X_{1t}, X_{2t} does not have the property and so the equation can balance. For example, both Xs could contain seasonals, but they might just match so that $b_1 X_{1t} + b_2 X_{2t}$ has no seasonal. The various possibilities are shown in Table 1.2.

If the dominant property is the unit root, or persistence, the case where a pair of Xs have the property but a linear

Table 1.2

P = has dominant property		B = equation balanced	
NP = does not have this property		NB = equation not balanced	

		X_1, X_2 both P	X_1, X_2 both NP	X_1, X_2 one P, one NP
Y	P	B	NB	B
	NP	NB?	B	NB

Note: NB? Will be NB unless there exists a linear combination of Xs which is NP.

$$Y_t = b_1 X_{1t} + b_2 X_{2t} + \text{error} - (\text{assumes error is } NP)$$

combination does not have it is found to occur quite frequently in economic time series, and is given the name "cointegration."

There can be a problem with a balanced set of variables on some occasions when an apparent relationship is found when truly none is present. This is well known to occur between a pair of smooth, or persistent, time series that are actually independent of each other but are modeled using standard techniques, in which case so-called "spurious relationships" can occur. Once one is aware of the possibility, appropriate techniques can be employed to avoid the difficulty.

A similar difficulty can occur with panel data. Suppose that X_{jt}, Y_{jt} are series measured at time t for the jth region, that each depend heavily on some measure of the "size" of the regions, such as area, population, wealth, or total income, and that this size varies greatly across regions, as occurs with actual US states or member countries of the UN. If one runs a regression explaining X_t by Y_t then a relationship will be "found" due to the missing size link and so a spurious relationship found. A particularly obvious case relates X_t to X_{t-1}, in which one is inclined to get what may be called "spurious stochastics" and thus biased forecasts. Again, there are several techniques available to reduce the importance of this problem.

Further problems with specification

To continue illustrating the difficulties faced in practice when specifying a model, consider just the simple form

$$Y_t = a + b_1 X_{1t} + b_2 X_{2t} + \ldots b_q X_{qt} + e_t.$$

Usually it is not sufficient to consider just a single equation as a system is required, but I am avoiding matrix analysis. The obvious decisions that have to be made include:

(i) what dependent variable Y_t to use, particularly what functional form; and

(ii) what explanatory variables, X_{jt} to include, with what lags, and involving what functional forms?

The Xs can include lagged Ys or functions of them. These decisions will be helped by consideration of the objectives of the model, by a pre-analysis of the series to determine their

Table 1.3 *Demand for newly cleared land*

Dependent variable: ΔCLR_t

Explaining variable	Coefficient	t-value
Constant	2.879	6.9
Distance to federal capital	−0.237	−5.3
Road length$_{t-1}$	0.047	5.0
Neighbors' changing in clearing$_t$	0.281	6.4
Rural pop. density$_{t-1}$	−0.002	−2.7
Level of clearing$_{t-1}$	−0.325	−15.9
Growth of urban output$_t$	0.095	2.8
Land price$_{t-1}$	−0.097	−4.5
Cattle herd$_{t-1}$	0.149	10.6
Change in cattle herd$_t$	0.267	11.2
Change in agricultural output$_t$	0.164	4.4
Change in land prices$_t$	−0.280	−11.6
Dummy for Mato Grosso	0.168	2.7
Number of observations	831	
Adjusted R^2	0.486	

major properties, both individually and also jointly for the
*X*s, and how a balanced equation can be achieved.

Let us return to consideration of the dynamics of
deforestation in Brazil. To complete the set of transition
equations discussed above, a demand equation for new
cleared land is required. An obvious choice for the dependent variable Y_t is the change in the amount of cleared land
in the region (ΔCLR_t) but alternatives that could be considered are ΔCLR_t/population or total area cleared at time *t* or
a growth rate, $\Delta CLR_t / CLR_{t-1}$. There are many possible

explanatory variables suggested by simple theory, by common sense, or used as proxies for important missing variables. Table 1.3 shows an estimated equation for ΔCLR_t using a constant and twelve explanatory variables including a dummy. The estimates use ordinary least squares, the least sophisticated estimation method available and also the easiest to appreciate. Shown are the coefficient estimates and the corresponding t-statistics. The original specification had included more explanatory variables, but those found to be "statistically insignificant" have been dropped from the model as shown. This is part of a "general" to "simple" strategy that is widely used and has some sound statistical justification. The variables so deleted include river length$_t$, distance to state capital$_t$, growth pole dummy$_i$, SUDAM credit$_{i,t-1}$, rural income per rural capita$_{i,t-1}$ and municipality area, for the ith municipality at the tth periods. As is usual with such regressions, some results are considered "sensible" and not surprising – such as demand decreasing with distance from the federal capital – some results might be considered surprising – demand increasing as neighboring areas clear more land – and some results are disappointing – the "policy variables" not coming into the model significantly. It follows that the model cannot be used directly in its present form to consider the effects of policy changes. However the model in table 1.3, which is taken from Andersen (1997), is part of a system and it is found that one of the inputs to ΔCLR_t, the growth in urban output$_t$, has SUDAM credit$_{t-1}$ as a significant input, and so it is seen that policy does have a two-stage and positive effect, resulting in an increase in demand for newly cleared land. The policy towards road building clearly has a direct positive effect, as seen in table 1.3 (t-values are shown rather than standard errors because they were provided in the original paper).

Some of the important, significant variables in the table have been interpreted by Andersen (1997) in terms of:

 (i) accessibility: such as distance to federal capital, road length, clearing in neighboring regions;
 (ii) saturation effects: lagged effects of clearing or as level gets high there is less available to clear;
 (iii) price effects: reflecting that much of the clearing takes place in frontier areas where land prices are low; and
 (iv) demand for grazing by the cattle industry: cattle herd size and change in this variable enter significantly.

This may not be the best specification available and the possibility of spurious relationships remains although the fact that municipality area was tried as an explanatory variable but not found to be relevant is supportive.

An obvious difficulty with such equations that several authors have raised is that of "data-mining" in which several different specifications are tried until the best one is found, but then just this best model is presented for our perusal without admitting that the other specifications had been considered. With modern computer power, and only 30 or 40 explanatory variables, such a search over possible models is easily achieved. I am certainly not suggesting that this occurred with the Brazilian data; in fact I know that it did not, but clearly such things can occur and they would be quite difficult to detect if just in-sample evaluation methods are used. Other possibilities will be discussed in chapter 2. Although methodologists sometimes consider such a "specification search" to be a potentially large problem, I am less pessimistic. A list of sensible explanatory variables will give a fit at a certain level and it is usually difficult to achieve a spurious fit of a significantly higher level merely by adding further randomly selected variables or more lags of a previously used variable, if the degree of freedom stays large, that is, if the amount of data points minus coefficients being estimated remains large. There are some cases where model fit is slightly improved by adding many more variables or lags, but the decisions based on these extended models are likely to be little different from those based on simpler, more parsimonious models. Problems can arise when very rich non-linear specifications are considered, but discussion of such topics could take me on too long a diversion, so I will avoid it.

The results of the Brazil deforestation models suggest that in about 80 years time there will be virtually no virgin rain forest remaining in the Amazon region of Brazil if present tendencies continue. Most of the land will have been converted to pasture or fallow which can, at best, be used for cattle or sheep ranching. These are activities that require a lot of space, generate little employment, and have low productivity. Lost will be thousands of animals and plant species, and millions of insect species that cannot be found elsewhere on the earth. The main policy variable for controlling this activity at this time is the building of new roads.

What should occur next is a cost/benefit analysis of a policy that encourages or discourages deforestation. A number of development economists attempt such calculations although they are inherently uncertain, as it is difficult to know the potential value of plant or insect species that have not yet been studied and which could have medical or bio-chemical benefits to mankind in the future, for example. One also has to weigh the current benefits to farmers in Brazil to the hypothetical costs to future generations, using an uncertain discount rate. Andersen (1997) has estimated that the present value benefit from deforestation is about $20,000 per hectare and that the cost (including lost sustainable logging, ecological services, bio-diversity loss, carbon release to the atmosphere, etc.) is about $18,000 per hectare. However, both of these estimates should be associated with high levels of uncertainty. Most economists strongly believe that further deforestation should be discouraged, but how the process of discouragement should be paid for, internationally, is unclear. The types of empirical results presented above help to place some of this discussion on a firmer, numerical foundation.

Looking forward and looking back

All intellectual pursuits evolve with time and it is easy to suggest that empirical modeling is about to undergo a period of rapid change, even one that can be considered a structural break in terms of our strategies and techniques. To put this into context, we can start by considering the methods used in the time that Alfred Marshall was Professor of Political Economy at Cambridge, from 1888 to 1908, about a century ago. In his writings he made it clear that he thoroughly approved of the idea of empirically testing theories and was frustrated by the lack of data and of appropriate techniques. As the years passed the quantity and quality of data improved, as did the speed and flexibility of the machinery available for computing and because of these changes more sophisticated econometric techniques were developed. During this evolution knowledge accumulated about the statistical properties of economic data, on what models appear to be successful and which can be discarded and on what are sensible, pragmatic modeling strategies. A hundred years may seem like a long time for knowledge to be passed on, but it only represents one linking generation. Alfred Marshall taught and was a colleague of John Maynard Keynes, who died in 1966. There are plenty of people now at Cambridge who were taught by or worked with Keynes, and so ideas and attitudes can easily be passed through the years.

One difficulty that economics has is that lessons learnt in one period may not always be applicable in a later period, if the structure of the economy changes enough. A structural change can take many forms, in some occasions virtually all the rules of the economy change, such as from communist to post-communist Russia, in others there may be changes to large parts of the economy but not all, as when Germany re-unified, or just certain sectors could be affected, such as in 1974 around the first OPEC price shock, which largely had impact on prices and the energy sector. Economies often are impacted by structural changes, mostly small policy or legal changes; but occasionally large ones. These changes need not be sudden and can occur over several years, but the structures pre- and post- the change may be quite different.

The deforestation model for the Amazon could face structural changes as government politics change, and thus their policies, as population pressures build up in other parts of the country, and as forests decline virtually to zero in other parts of Brazil. These can be partially allowed for in the model by the use of year dummies, but exploration of the possibilities of other parameters changing through time would also be worthwhile.

Why modeling in general is facing such a change is partly because of the advances being made in computing speed and memory but also because of the appearance of very large data sets in economics, which were very rare in the past.

Over my own research life, of about forty years, I have experienced computer speeds increasing from at most one calculation every ten seconds, on an electric desk calculator, to current speeds of perhaps one billion calculations per second. A new computer has just started running at a thousand times faster than that. Very approximately, every year computer speed increases about 20 percent and memory capabilities increase by roughly 40 percent. These represent exponential growths and can be compared to a 3 percent growth in GDP for the typical developed country or about 10 percent for a very successful developing country. We are rapidly reaching the situation where there are no technical constraints and very few cost constraints on us performing any statistical calculation needed for economic modeling.

Computers can already handle very large data sets, which is appropriate as these are now becoming available in economics, largely due to electronic data collection and recording devices. Some examples are:

(i) the price and volume of every transaction on a stock market, such as London or the New York Stock Exchange, over a week, producing one to four million numbers. These values are now recorded for every exchange around the world and soon there will be several years worth of figures, about two thousand million numbers (2 billion US);

(ii) every transaction on a particular brand of credit card is recorded and instantaneously relayed to a central office for analysis to search for trends or for improper use of cards. In Europe or the United States this would each be over 1 million observations per day;

(iii) almost every item bought in a supermarket is recorded by the use of bar-codes, so that what is being bought, where, at what price, and with what other items, can be analyzed. If payment is made with a credit card it is possible to link the purchases with various household characteristics of the card-owner, such as income level, own or rent a house or apartment, single or married, etc. The quality of data is truly enormous when the data from all these stores is put together.

There are other examples but most arise from micro-economics and finance, however even in macro it is now possible to get interest-rates daily over a wide range of terms, money supply daily, and several important series weekly, so changes are happening. Even though a series such as GDP is available only quarterly, largely due to the costs of collecting the basic data from which it is constructed, it is possible to estimate what GDP would have been if it had been measured monthly – a "virtual monthly GDP" – with these monthly values being regularly calibrated against the observed quarterly figures. In theory, this can be extended to shorter periods.

The availability of these large data sets means that new statistical modeling techniques have to be devised to take advantage of them and many of the classical techniques can be discarded, as they were developed for small data sets devised from biological or agricultural experimental situations. Assumptions of linear relationships and thus also of normality can certainly be dropped and ways of estimating and interpreting conditional distributions will have to be found. Essentially, many of the tools you are currently learning in statistics and econometrics will not be needed in the future, although the foundations and strategies you are being taught should certainly remain helpful. As a simple example for a very large data set virtually every precise null hypothesis will be rejected using standard significance levels, unless the hypothesis is exactly correct. We will be able to place more emphasis on economic significance rather than statistical significance when interpreting our results. It follows, I believe, that the economist will have to be much more precise about the objectives of the theory or modeling process, which leads me to chapter 2.

References

Andersen, L.E. (1997), "Modeling the Relationship Between Government Policy, Economic Growth, and Deforestation in the Brazilian Amazon." Working paper 1997–2, Department of Economics, University of Aarhus, Denmark.

Rezili, J. and A. Ozanne (1997), "An Error Correction Model of Output Supply and Input Demand in Greek Agriculture." Working paper 9705, School of Economic Studies, University of Manchester.

Stigum, B. (1990), *Towards A Formal Science of Economics*. MIT Press: Cambridge, MA.

Stigum, B. (1995), "Theory-data Confrontations in Economics." *Dialogue* 34, 581–604, Canadian Philosophical Association.

Further reading

Banerjee, A., J. Dolado, J.W. Galbraith, and D. Hendry (1993), *Cointegration, Error-Correction, and the Econometric Analysis of Non-stationary Data*. Oxford University Press.

Granger, C.W.J. (1990), *Modeling Economic Series*. Oxford University Press.

Hatanaka, M. (1996), *Time Series Based Econometrics*. Oxford University Press.

Hendry, D. (1995), *Dynamic Econometrics*. Oxford University Press.

CHAPTER TWO

The evaluation of empirical models

General comments

How do I know if an economic theory or an empirical model is any good? This is an important question that is asked insufficiently often in published reports and papers. Anyone can write down a piece of theory or present an empirical model and propose that it be used, but how do we know that the model or theory has any worthwhile content? This is the type of question that I will explore in this chapter.

When the word "evaluate" was introduced in the mid nineteenth century, according to the *Concise Oxford English Dictionary* it meant to put a numerical value on to something. However, the quotation that the dictionary used to illustrate the word was from the famous biologist J.S. Huxley, "to read all previous work on the subject, in order evaluate one's own results correctly." Now the word is being used in a subjective rather than a quantitative way. Frequently evaluations will involve a comparison between alternatives, and possibly even a ranking, but this does not necessarily involve strict cardinal measurements.

It is worthwhile starting out by considering evaluation in a general context. Society at large appears to have a mixed attitude toward evaluation; some sections seem to use it a great deal, other parts quite rarely, at least publically.

Doctors and dentists evaluate patients, engineers evaluate bridges, and teachers evaluate students. Here, there is some certification that the person performing the evaluation is qualified to do so. In newspapers critics evaluate films, music, and books; elsewhere stock-brokers evaluate companies, real estate agents evaluate houses and commercial buildings, and, in many universities, students evaluate teachers. The competence of the evaluators is now less clear and the natural question to arise is – how do we evaluate the evaluations?

Whenever there is widespread, direct competition that can be observed sufficient information is usually generated to deduce a ranking of the alternatives. Most sporting activities provide examples if there are enough competitions, so that rankings are fairly easy to achieve even worldwide. Soccer or rugby are examples, but less so in boxing or angling. In sport, competition provides the evaluation, and the same could be said for goods or companies involved in active markets. A product that sells well may be considered to be ranked higher than one that has lower sales, and a film with large box-office sales is more successful than one that sells less tickets. In a sense, evaluation here is by use of an economic measure. Of course, there are other methods of evaluation of these products which do not correspond to purely economic measurements. Publications such as *Which* and *Consumer's Reports* attempt to measure the "quality" of consumer products, at least on an ordinal scale. Film critics, similarly, discuss quality. There is often not a strong relationship between the market evaluations and the alternative quality-based ones, as is seen from the fact that previous top-selling films such as *ET* and the *Star Wars* trilogy did not win Oscars although *Titanic* was successful. It should be noted that the evaluations are actually on different objects, the sales will be affected by the quality of the product, its price, plus the marketing effort surrounding it whereas the critics will be less concerned by price or marketing. The critics will claim to be influenced only by "quality," even though this concept is difficult to define or even discuss, which is why they may not agree.

In other parts of society there is little evidence of evaluation, or at least if it occurs the results are not publicized. I have not seen evaluations of judges, dentists, lawyers, or university administrators, for example. At the other extreme, prominent politicians are continually being evaluated and criticized, within the media or at elections, which is a truly formidable type of evaluation.

University teachers and professors are frequently evaluated, particularly in the United States, for their teaching and research abilities and for their general service to the department, university, and the profession at large. The teaching evaluation is all too frequently based on the results of surveys of the students they have taught. It is generally recognized that students may not be well qualified as critics of their teachers; they can certainly comment on technical aspects such as clarity but less so on the course contents as they may not know if the course is unbiased and up-to-date? The people best qualified to evaluate the teacher are not the students but those who eventually employ the students, although the question of how value-added is measured is a difficult one.

What I think is clear from this initial discussion is that in society at large evaluation may or may not occur, there is a difficulty in deciding on the criterion used to rank competitors, alternative evaluations can occur and they may well not agree as they use different criteria, and that rarely are evaluations themselves evaluated. Now let us now turn to consideration of evaluation in economics.

Evaluation in economics

At first glance, economics is an intellectual area that pays little attention to the question of evaluation. As evidence I place the following facts:

(i) In the first 28 volumes of the *Handbook of Economics* (published by North-Holland/Elsevier) containing about 15 thousand pages, the combined indices only make two mentions of evaluation. One is to a brief statement in a chapter on input–output tables but with no discussion and the other is to a section in a chapter of which I was a co-author.

(ii) *The New Palgrave, A Dictionary of Economics* (1987, Macmillan Press) contains 2,000 entries by 900 contributors in 4,000 pages. The index contains 3,000 items but does not mention "evaluation."

This is not to say that the topic did not arise in some form within these books, possibly using synonyms such as "validation," just that it was not emphasized sufficiently to get into the indices more frequently.

As we all know, evaluation in some form is a central feature of many parts of economics. Consumers are taken to make their decisions so as to attain the highest available utility; companies maximize profits or returns when making decisions; on any speculative market assets are ranked according to their expected returns after allowing for risks; and forecasts are evaluated in terms of their relative quality. What is perhaps surprising is that these approaches are not used everywhere in economics.

Let me give you an example. It is hypothetical to make it easier to contemplate, but is also based on discussions with a number of colleagues. Suppose that I need a particular statistic to help me make an economic decision. The statistic I require is, say, the elasticity of demand for watermelons in a particular region of the US. I will suppose that there is a relevant set of cross-sectional data that can be used for the construction of an econometric model for watermelons. In passing, it might be noted that one of the classical pieces of econometric modeling considered just this topic (Suits (1955)). If the data were given to four different econometricians almost certainly they would use different specifications and build four different models and thus derive four estimates of the elasticity I require, $\lambda_1, \lambda_2, \lambda_3$, and λ_4. How do I decide which λ to use in my decision? In these circumstances an econometrician will almost invariably start to consider the relative qualities of the models that produced the estimates, asking which best fitted the data, which had a specification founded on theory of good quality, which used a sound estimation procedure that had been shown to be consistent or superior under some criterion, and so forth. In other words, the belief is that the best estimates of an elasticity will come from the model that, in some way, is the best. Let us stop for a moment and ask: is this reasoning necessarily correct?

Let me first consider a painting. If an art critic is asked an opinion of the quality of the "op-art" piece entitled "Green–Blue–Red" by Ellsworth Kelly, 1964, does the critic start by asking what type of canvas was used, what type of paints and brushes? When considering the quality of a painting we pay little attention to the quality of the materials used to make it. This is not true of all art, particularly sculpture. Similarly, one can ask: do you evaluate a university by the quality of its classrooms or by the quality of its graduates? In all of these examples, it is surely the quality of the **output** that is of prime importance. In some special areas there seems to be a strong belief that it takes a great input to produce a great output, cigars and wine are obvious examples. It might be claimed that it is impossible to produce a great wine of a certain variety without using grapes of high quality from a very specific region, although it is admitted that these grapes can be used to produce quite ordinary wine on occasions. There is, however, a vanity effect that purchasers may experience; they obtain a higher utility just from knowing the reputation the brand has for high quality or from the high price paid for the commodity, compared to the utility they would obtain directly from the commodity if tested "blind." There is absolutely nothing wrong with such vanity effects, which help explain the sales of many expensive watches, cars and bottles of foreign water around the world, but they represent just a few special examples.

In the cases just considered there may be several groups each evaluating the same object (piece of art), person (teacher), or commodity (cigar). For the art work there will be the artist, the art critic working for a magazine, the art museum curator, and the public, all with quite different viewpoints. Returning to consideration of the alternative estimates of the elasticity of demand for watermelons, there will be two quite different groups interested in evaluation: the producers of the models and the consumers of their output, in this case the estimates. The producers will be interested in the quality of the models but the consumers in the quality of the outputs, the decision maker will want to use the best estimate. One group will look at the models, which may be thought of as an intermediate good, the other group just at the outputs. How this is done will be discussed later.

It could be argued that if you are too familiar with the model, you may not take the output sufficiently seriously. For example the bible suggests that Jesus, on His return from 20 years wandering in the wilderness, had great success spreading His new and original ideas, except at Nazareth which is the village where He spent His youth and where He was personally well known. It was easier for people who did not know Him to accept the ideas than people who had known Him when young.

A difficulty with evaluating a piece of art is that it is not supposed to be useful in any particular way or even give increased utility to the public at large. The same will be true for a piece of pure mathematics research. It will have originality and possibly even a beauty in itself, but this will be appreciated by few and its uses elsewhere may never occur or not for many years. I would argue that most economic research should not want to be considered to be like pure mathematics but should be associated with a clear-cut and precisely stated objective. Only by knowing the proposed purpose or planned use of a theory or model can it be evaluated. It is difficult to imagine a scientist starting a complicated experiment without having a plan or a purpose for its outcome. However, some pieces of economic research start out with a vague objective, such as "explaining" or "understanding" some economic occurrence or relationship. The question arises, how does the researcher know when such an objective has been reached? I certainly do not intend to discuss a deep and controversial topic such as "What economists should do" but I am amazed that some methodologists appear to be content with economics providing an "explanation" for what has occurred in the past. The difficulty is that generally there is not a unique explanation for a particular historical event. It is thus impossible to distinguish which, if any, of the alternative explanations is correct. Precisely the same argument applies with models that explain a small set of "stylized facts." Initially it is interesting to know that there exists a model which can do it but once several alternative models become available then a different criteria is needed to choose between them. Many pieces of research claim to have successfully "explained" some event or phenomenon or to allow the economists to "understand" some situation. An an analogy, consider being given a new piece of electronic equipment and a book of instructions. After reading the instructions a person may claim to understand them but the proof will occur if that person can actually use the equipment correctly, or as promised when it was originally obtained.

There are many statistical measures of the goodness of fit of a model based on the in-sample data, which are the same data that were used for a specification search and for estimation. For various reasons this model may be over-fitted. One finds these days, for instance, that models used in policy debates are formed by groups advocating different policy positions, and it is likely that specifications have been chosen to put their positions in the best light possible. An out-of-sample evaluation clearly is going to provide a less-biased comparison; it is much more difficult to bias post-sample performance than in-sample unless there is some real quality to your case. This point is amplified later where a variety of realistic questions are discussed.

To discuss the problems faced when attempting to evaluate, or test, a specific theory, I now turn to consideration of Hall's theory of consumption, as an example.

Testing Hall's theory of consumption

In 1978 Robert Hall discussed the stochastic implications of jointly considering two well-known pieces of economic theory, one concerned with consumption decisions over the life cycle and the other the permanent income hypothesis. Putting these together he showed that a number of surprising and potentially interesting simple results could be derived, using the following notation:

δ rate of subjective time preference, so that £1 now and £$(1 + \delta)1$ next period are equally acceptable.

r real rate of interest.

$u(\ )$ is a one-period utility function for the consumer considered.

c_t consumption by the consumer in period t.

E_t mathematical expectation conditional on all information available at time t.

r is assumed to be constant and $\geq \delta$.

For an individual consumer, the basic theorem says that if the consumer maximizes expected utility then

$$E_t u'(c_{t+1}) = [(1 + \delta)/(1 + r)]u'(c_t)$$

where $u'(c) = du(c)/dc$. Some corollaries to the theorem are particularly interesting.

(i)   "no information available in period t, apart from the level of consumption, c_t, helps predict future consumption, c_{t+1}, in the sense of affecting the expected value of marginal utility. In particular, income or wealth in periods t or earlier are irrelevant, once c_t is known" (Hall's words).

(ii) $u'(c_{t+1}) = \gamma u'(c_t) + \epsilon_{t+1}$ where $\gamma = (1 + \delta)/(1 + r)$ and ϵ_{t+1} is such that $E_t[\epsilon_{t+1}] = 0$.

(iii) if the utility function is quadratic, so that $u(c_t) = -(c_t - c_0)^2$ then $c_{t+1} = \beta + \gamma c_t - \epsilon_{t+1}$ and if the utility function has the constant elasticity of substitution form $u(c_t) = c_t^{(\sigma - 1)/\sigma}$ then $c_{t+1}^\lambda = \gamma c_t^\lambda + \epsilon_{t+1}$, $\lambda = -\sigma^{-1}$.

This theory was like manna from heaven to macroeconometricians. It was easily stated and understood and appears to be easy to test. Testing becomes particularly simple with the quadratic utility function and with the expectation that γ will be near one and so the theory gives for consumption a random walk, possibly with small drift.

$$c_{t+1} = \beta_0 + c_t + e_{t+1}. \tag{1}$$

All we need to do now is to gather some data and test this model.

However, the initial empirical models did not completely support the theory and it is interesting to ask why. One major reason is that actual consumption data are highly seasonal, with large values around Christmas, and this property of the data is not anticipated by the theory. It is possible to argue that the theory was taking a long-run viewpoint whereas seasonality is a short-run component, and it is clear that the theory can be altered in sensible ways to account for it. If one uses seasonally adjusted data this difficulty is reduced although possibly other problems are introduced. Studies have found that seasonal adjustment can produce loss of information, can introduce non-linearity, and can induce seasonality in volatility, for example.

It is usual to denote "change in c_t" by $\Delta c_t \equiv c_t - c_{t-1}$ and then the simplest implications of the theory says

$$\Delta c_t = \beta + \epsilon_t \tag{2}$$

where β is a small or zero constant and ϵ_t is white noise, and so cannot be forecast from its own past – and the theory actually says that it cannot be forecast at all! We can easily test equation (2) by embedding it in a wider class of models. For example

$$\Delta c_t = \beta + \alpha_1 \Delta c_{t-1} + \alpha_2 \Delta c_{t-2} + \epsilon_t$$

and asking if $\alpha_1 = 0$ and $\alpha_2 = 0$.

If the answer is, apparently yes – so that α_1, α_2 are not significantly different from zero – that would appear to be evidence in favor of the theory. However, before accepting even that, one has to question the interpretation of the case when α_1 or α_2 are not zero, as was found in some of the initial tests of the theory. Is this evidence against the theory? Not necessarily, as the theory has not been stated clearly enough. When lags of one time unit are mentioned in the theory, the definition of **one** time unit is not defined or discussed. This time unit for decisions may well not be the same time unit over which the data have been gathered – usually quarterly. Does one really believe that consumers condition their consumption decisions only on data available thirteen weeks previously? There is an old theorem, due to an economist who worked on commodities, Halbrook Working (1960), which says if a stock series is generated by a random walk over one time interval but actually is observed over a longer time interval of m units then the change series will be a moving average of the form $\epsilon_t + b\epsilon_{t-1}$ where

$$\frac{b}{1 + b^2} = \frac{m^2 - 1}{2(2m^2 + 1)}.$$

Using US consumption of services and non-durable goods (quarterly, seasonally adjusted, constant 1972 dollars, 1947-I to 1984-III) Ermini (1988) estimates the model

$$\Delta c_t = \epsilon_t + 0.239\epsilon_{t-1}. \tag{3}$$

Various more complicated models, with lags of Δc_t and further lagged ϵ_t terms included, were considered but not found to give significantly better likelihood values. The pure random walk model was also rejected against this change and moving average. At face value, this model rejects the Hall theory if the decision time period is a quarter, but, using Working's result, it is consistent with Hall's theory if the decision period is rather shorter than a quarter. Using the estimated coefficient of 0.239, a value of m can be solved to give $m = 6$, corresponding to a decision time unit of roughly two weeks. The process of starting with a model over one time unit but observing data from it over a longer unit is known as temporal aggregation. What is seen here is that Hall's theory, with no specific time unit, is consistent with some of the empirical results plus temporal aggregation. Although certainly good news for the theory this information is not convincing evidence for it, as several other models will also temporarily aggregate into the same model (3), including changes with moving average terms with negative coefficients and larger m values.

Although Hall's theory was for an individual consumer, the majority of the data used to test it consists of macro, aggregate data; that is the sum of consumption figures over many individuals, perhaps nearly 100 million in the United States.

If the basic form of the theory were to hold for *every* individual

$$\Delta c_{jt} = \beta_j + \epsilon_{jt} \text{ for } j\text{th individual} \qquad (4)$$

then in the aggregate

$$\Delta \bar{c}_t = \bar{\beta} + \bar{\epsilon}_t \qquad (5)$$

where the bar indicates a sum or aggregate. However, the reverse is not true, (5) could hold for the aggregate but (4) not hold for individuals. The algebra is somewhat complicated and will not be shown here but can be found in Granger (1987). Thus, strictly, the Hall theory cannot be tested using aggregate data.

A further example of that is found from consideration of the non-quadratic utility function. If one wanted to test the form of the theory

$$c_t^\lambda = \beta + c_{t-1}^\lambda + \epsilon_t$$

then the variable sum over individuals of c_{jt}^λ is not available at the aggregate level for $\lambda \neq 1$, and is only slightly related to the variable

(sum over all individuals of consumption)$^\lambda$.

One last prediction of the theory that is difficult to test is that Δc_t cannot be forecast by any variable. Suppose that this proposition were correct, it would be possible to accumulate evidence in its favor by trying a number of plausible variables and finding that they did not, in fact, help forecast but it would clearly be impossible to try all economic variables that are considered to be of relevance.

It is seen that even such an apparently simple theory as Hall's is difficult to phrase properly, to find correct data for it and formulate appropriate strong tests. Of course it is possible to reject the theory, thereby allowing a stronger theory to be evolved and it is possible to show the ways in which the theory does give an interesting approximation to reality, thus showing its strengths, but a final evaluation is not simple to construct. There is a considerable literature suggesting rejection of the theory for various other reasons than those discussed above, which is hardly surprising for such a simple theory.

Hall's original paper was not very clear about the objectives of the theory. It is stated that the paper asks "exactly what can be learnt from a consumption regression when . . . none of the 'explanatory' variables are exogenous." The account then goes on to discuss how to test the theoretical implications of the work. However, the paper does finish with a discussion of the implications of the theory, if correct, for macroeconomic forecasting and policy analysis and so one might deduce that those are the true, practical purposes of the theory. It will be thus appropriate to turn to consideration of evaluation in the fields of forecasting, policy, and finance.

Evaluation of forecasts and in finance

In the area of forecasting, evaluation is well developed but still requires further thought. A simplified version will be considered here, where a single series X_t is, at time n, being forecast h steps ahead, based on an information set I_n, which will consist of several explanatory variables including X_n and past values X_{n-j}, $j > 0$. Only information known at time n will be in I_n and can be used to form a forecast, and only numerical information is considered. Thus expectations of the future can be in I_n, if they are based on variables already in I_n but do use actual future values.

Standing at time n, the future value X_{n+h} is a random variable and thus will have a conditional distribution or probability distribution function $P_n(x|I_n) \equiv \mathrm{Prob}$ $(X_{n+h} \leq x|I_n)$. This distribution tells us everything we can about a future random variable; it fully characterizes it and from it we can get any summary statistic we might want, such as conditional means, variances, medians, quantiles, and so forth. There is often a need for a single statistic, called a "point forecast" $f_{n,h}$, which summarizes the location of the conditional distribution and is a function of the contents of I_n. The resulting "forecast error" is defined by

$$e_{n,h} = X_{n+h} - f_{n,h},$$

that is the value that actually occurs minus the point forecast. If a decision is based on the point forecast the costs will arise from the fact that the perfect point forecast is not always used. Suppose that the costs are just some function of the size of the errors, $C(e)$. Sensible properties for this cost function are that $C(0) = 0$ and it increases monotonically from zero, so that $C(e_1) > C(e_2)$ if $e_1 < e_2 < 0$ or if $e_1 > e_2 > 0$.

There is no reason why the cost function should be symmetric, in fact often the cost of making a negative error is quite different than making a positive error of the same size. Think about getting to the airport (or even to a lecture!) 10 minutes late rather than 10 minutes early. The point forecast is chosen so that the expected cost is minimized, which is formally stated by

$$\min_{f} \int C(x - f_{n,h}) dP_n(x|I_n).$$

For many cost functions, this integral is difficult to solve analytically, but can always be solved numerically. Given the point forecast, the errors $e_{n,h}$ will be observed at time $n + h$ and thus the associated costs $C(e_{n,h})$ arise. For any particular model or theory, a set of predictive distributions, point forecasts, and errors, and thus average costs, can be derived. The model generating the lowest average cost will be preferred and this preference is based on an economic measure.

The sequence to produce a point forecast is to find the conditional distribution produced by the "modeler" $\rightarrow P_n(X_{n+h}|I_n)$, insert the cost function to be used to evaluate as given by the "consumer" $\rightarrow C(e)$, then solve the equation to get the forecast $f_{n,h}$.

What is often done now is that the producer assumes that the cost function is just $C(e) = Ae^2$, and $A > 0$, which gives $f_{n,h} = $ conditional mean $P_n(X_{n+h}|I_n)$, so the producer merely has to provide the conditional mean rather than the whole conditional distribution. However, if actual consumers have different cost functions, the producer of models is forced to provide the complete conditional distribution and also a program to solve the integral for the particular cost function used by the consumer. It will still be possible that certain forecasting methods will be superior under some cost functions but not under others.

For example, Steve Satchell and Allan Timmermann reported in 1995 that linear methods of forecasting foreign exchange rates performed better than a simple non-linear switching trading strategy according to a squared cost function but less well for a measure based on the values of returns from portfolios generated by the alternative trading rules. Fifteen daily exchange rates were considered for 13 years, giving 3,393 observations. The economic value measure is surely the one that is of the greatest relevance to an economist and for these data the non-linear switching rule provided the greatest "end wealth" for a hypothetical portfolio in twelve of the fifteen cases, with the linear predictions generally beating a simple "buy-and-hold" strategy.

This example illustrates not only the advantages of using an economic measure to evaluate a model's performance rather than a statistical one, but also the wide-spread use of such measures in the financial literature. The success of a theory or model can be directly measured by the distribution of returns from a portfolio selected from it. If average returns are identical, the distribution of returns of the portfolio from an alternative model can be compared by tests using a deeper concept known as "stochastic dominance," which essentially asks if one variable is more uncertain than another.

The area of finance also teaches a further often important lesson about evaluation; it is not enough to evaluate a single entity (theory, model, stock, consumer product) by itself, as it has to be considered in terms of its value within a portfolio or bundle of goods. The point is, of course, familiar from the micro theory of consumption, where complementary goods take extra value when used in conjunction, such as coffee and cream for many people or toast and butter. This portfolio effect is particularly obvious with the choice of participants in a sports team, one would not want a cricket team consisting of just bowlers or a soccer team of just defenders or just goal keepers, however good they were. It is surprising how difficult it is to make this portfolio value case to university deans considering the tenure decision for a particular faculty member at a US university, for example.

Evaluation of policy models

Rene Magritte, the Surrealist painter, has a picture from 1929 titled "The Use of Words" showing a pipe for smoking above the words "Ceci n'est pas une pipe" (This is not a pipe). I am often reminded of this painting when I see economic models that claim to be policy models. It is common practice in the economic research literature to present a theory or empirical model and then have a final section discussing the "policy implications of the results." It is virtually never pointed out that the policy implications only hold if the model or theory is completely correct, which is an unlikely situation. The authors need to do more than to make the statement "This is a policy model" and assume others will accept the statement and thus the conclusions from the model. Policy models can be used to produce conditional forecasts. If I change a variable X that is in my control from X_A to X_B then at a specified time in the future Y will change from Y_A to Y_B. The actual values expected for Y_A, Y_B may depend on the current values taken by a number of other economic variables if a sufficiently complicated model is used.

An obvious difficulty with policy models is that usually one is not allowed to experiment with different policies to observe if the outcomes are as predicted by the model, so that evaluation of these models cannot be conducted in exactly the same way as with forecasting models, where the output is compared to the actual outcomes by the use of a cost function. However, the economy may well conduct a few "natural experiments" for us during the observed data set, the control variables will change and one can ask if the conditional forecasts from the model, knowing the future value of the control variable, are closer to the actual outcome for the variable of interest compared to the fore-casts not knowing the future of the control variable. If the answer is positive, the model will have passed a simple test and it remains a plausible candidate for a control model, otherwise there is a reduction in its claims to be a model useful for considering controls, at least similar to those that have actually occurred in the past.

As opposed to changes just in the policy variable, there are occasionally changes in the policy rule. This may be considered a structural break in the way in which the value for the policy variable is chosen each period and corresponds to changes in parameter values of the equation for this rule. In a well-known comment known as the "Lucas critique," it was correctly suggested that this parameter instability will be likely to cause parameters to change in some of the behavioral equations of the model. Any equation whose parameters do not change as the policy rule changes have been called "super-exogenous" and this property can be tested. These tests will then suggest the limits to the effects in the model of the change in the policy rule. From the viewpoint of accumulated experience it seems that the Lucas critique is of more importance in theory than in practice. Generally, the question of how to evaluate policy models, which is a very important one, is undeveloped in econometrics. References to recent work in the area are in Banerjee and Hendry (1997).

Some conclusions

When Professor Pesaran, with his colleague Dr. Smith (1985), considered the evaluation of macroeconometric models they suggested three criteria: Relevance, Consistency, and Adequacy.

By "Relevance," they meant that the model meets its required purpose.

By "Consistency," that it is consistent about what else is known about the area being modeled.

By "Adequacy," we have all the usual statistical measures of goodness of fit.

Although I agree that consistency and adequacy are important when building a model, that is searching over possible models, I will argue that a generalized form of relevance is of most use for evaluation.

Having discussed evaluation in those parts of economics where it is a prominent topic, let us return to consideration of the estimation of the elasticity of watermelons. These estimates are based on cross-section data sets, or possibly a panel. The claim made earlier was that most efforts on comparative evaluation of the alternative estimates would concentrate on the quality of the models that were constructed, using various statistical measures. More generally, attention may also be paid to the quality of the data used as inputs to the models if different data sets were used but here the same data set is assumed to be used in all cases. I would argue that we should evaluate the models by the quality of their outputs and by using economic measures. These are not exactly new points and I am certainly not claiming any originality. The proposal that theories should be evaluated in terms of economic values was one of the foundations of the group of philosophers called the "pragmatists" active at the turn of the century in the United States, whose ideas were best advocated by William James. Many of the ideas suggested by the pragmatists would, I believe, sound sensible to an economist, although they were being applied to a much wider range of topics than economic models and theories. When applied to questions such as the existence of God, they may seem less plausible. Other earlier similar stances on evaluation include Camilo Dagum (1989). He quotes the Spanish philosopher Juan Luis Vivres (1492–1560) who observed that "knowledge is of value only when it is put to use" and the economist Jacob Marshak (1953) who stated "knowledge is useful if it helps to make the best decisions . . ." Although these points have a long history they still do not seem to have impacted on the behavior of the majority of econometricians working outside the purely time series field. The format that is required is to specifically consider a real decision that is to be based on the elasticity estimation, and then ask if one can measure the cost, or benefit, in currency units of using one elasticity estimate rather than another? This would enable a ranking of the estimates to be obtained but it does require a passage of time from making the decision to the measurement of the economic consequences of the decision. However, with the addition of a few brave, untestable assumptions, an approximation to these quantities might be estimated from cross-section data. What seems to be currently missing is less the ability to evaluate in this type of area but the mind-set of thinking about outcome → decision → cost/benefit measurement.

To be operational, it is clear that the measure has to be directly observable and cannot be vague, such as "increased utility." It is also clear that an economic theory has to be evaluated in terms of its performance as measured by the actual economy, and thus by the use of data rather just on mathematical or intellectual grounds. This is a viewpoint that is accepted by an important group of theorists, although they still seem to be in the minority.

I would like to cite a pair of authorities that are very much better than myself. John Maynard Keynes, writing about Alfred Marshall says "Marshall arrived early at the point of view that the bare bones of economic theory are not worth much in themselves and do not carry one in the direction of useful, practical conclusions. The whole point lies in applying them to the interpretation of current economic life" (J.M. Keynes, "Memoir on Alfred Marshall, 1842–1924," *Economic Journal*, September 1924).

To paraphrase the position being taken here, a theory or model should be evaluated in terms of the quality of the decisions that are made based on the theory or model. If the model cannot be used to make decisions (if it is incomplete, for instance), then it should be considered to be an intermediate good rather than a final product and cannot be evaluated in the way that is being suggested here. It is inevitable that the decisions are made temporally later than the period over which the empirical model was specified and thus the evaluation is essentially "post-sample," rather than the usual "goodness-of-fit" in-sample which is now often used. A difficulty with using a post-sample evaluation approach is that if regime-switching occurs, the new data may be generated from a different process than the in-sample data. The implication is that the model will be of little use for decision making in the new regime and has to be evaluated accordingly. It could not be used for policy decisions, for example.

I would like to suggest that in the future, when you are presented with a new piece of theory or an empirical model, you ask these questions:

(i) What purpose does it have? What economic decision does it help with? and;

(ii) Is there any evidence being presented that allows me to evaluate its quality compared to alternative theories or models?

I believe that attention to such questions will strengthen economic research and discussion.

The evaluation process proposed here, by comparing the quality of the decisions based on a flow of outputs from competing models, is not always easy to implement. In particular, it cannot be applied to single, one-off events which will continue to be particularly difficult, perhaps impossible, to evaluate. I would like to illustrate this point with an appropriate example.

Suppose that an entrepreneur with a small business proposes a particular plan to make his enterprise successful. Further suppose that others with similar businesses all agree that the plan is very unlikely to succeed; indeed that he will lose money compared to them. It is possible that in most occasions the critics will be correct, but in a special case, which the entrepreneur believed was about to occur, his plan would be a great success. The evaluation is now not just of the plan but of the plan plus the timing of its implementation, and so no sequence of decisions can be based on it.

In my example suppose a farmer decides just to employ workers who are physically disadvantaged; or, in the words of an account written in the early part of this century, "he indulged in a certain eccentricity by seeking an advantage indirectly by refusing to employ anyone who did not suffer from some physical defect, staffing himself entirely with the halt, the blind, and the maimed." The reasons for this choice by the "pasturalist" may have been humanitarian but I prefer to believe that it was based on economic reasoning. It is part of a story that I suppose most students of economics at Cambridge are familiar with but students elsewhere may be less aware. The small farmer was Charles Marshall, the place was Australia, and the time was the middle of the nineteenth century, at the very start of the Australian gold rush. When the gold boom reached its height his reward came. His neighbors, who had laughed at his policy, lost all of their men but his was the only farm to carry on in a productive way and was thus very profitable.

Part of these profits went as a loan to his nephew, a young Cambridge Fellow at St. John's College, Alfred Marshall in 1861, enabling him to switch from a study of Theology and the Classics (and thus a career as a cleric) to the study of mathematics and thus providing one of the major growth points in the founding of mathematical economics.[1]

A rather minor consequence of that are the annual Marshall Lectures.

References

Banerjee, A. and D.F. Hendry (1997), *The Econometrics of Economic Policy*. Blackwell: Oxford.

Dagum, Camilo (1989), "Scientific Model Building: Principles, Methods and History." In *Theoretical Empiricism*, edited by Herman Wold. Paragon House: New York.

Ermini, Luigi (1988), "Temporal Aggregation and Hall's Model of Consumption Behavior." *Applied Economics* 20, 1317–20.

Granger, Clive W.J. (1987), "Implications of Aggregation With Common Factors." *Econometric Theory* 3, 208–222.

Hall, R. (1978), "Stochastic Implications of the Life-Cycle Permanent Income Hypothesis: Theory and Evidence." *Journal of Political Economy* 86, 971–987.

Marshak, J. (1953), "Economic Measurements For Policy and Prediction." In *Studies In Econometric Methods,* edited by W.H. Hood and T.C. Koopmans. Wiley and Sons: New York.

Pesaran, H. and R. Smith (1985), "Evaluation of Macroeconometric Models." *Economic Modeling,* April, 125–134.

Satchell, S. and Allan Timmermann (1995), "An Assessment of the Economic Value of Nonlinear Foreign Exchange Rate Forecasts." *Journal of Forecasting* 14, 477–497.

Suits, P.B. (1955), "An Econometric Model of the Watermelon Market." *Journal of Farm Economics* 37, 237–251.

Working, H. (1960), "Note on the Correlation of First Differences of Averages in a Random Chain." *Econometrica* 28, 916–198.

---

[1] Just before giving the lecture I was told that the story of Charles Marshall may have been less dramatic than it sounds; his farm workers were unable to leave and go to the gold fields because he often employed convicts who were limited in their movements.

CHAPTER THREE

Comments on the evaluation of econometric models and of forecasts

Plan of chapter

As this chapter contains material that is more technical than that used in the previous two essays, the form will be an unconventional one, with less formal sections discussing generally, but not precisely, what will be in the following formal sections. Thus section "1 INF" (for informal) will be informal and, hopefully, will help in the understanding of the context of the following section "1 FOR" (for formal). The chapter is discussing various approaches to the evaluation of econometric models and particularly of forecasts.

1 INF Is an empirical model worthwhile?

Econometricians and empirical modelers in economic fields spend a great deal of effort in constructing their models. Appropriate data are gathered, alternative specifications considered, a good dose of economic theory inserted and the model is carefully estimated. The final model is then ready to be presented to the public like some exotic dish in an expensive restaurant. Just looking at the model, the natural question arises – is it any good? Unfortunately, this question is not answered very often, or is not always taken very seriously. To approach the question, it is important for the purpose of the model to be clearly specified; again a statement of purpose is often not attached or is not sufficiently precise to be useful. Some parts of econometrics behave as though the purpose of the modeling exercise is to find a model that is well estimated and which appears to fit the data well, according to some criterion. However, the approach taken throughout this chapter is that the model should be useful to a decision maker. Thus the modeling exercise should be extended to include not only an evaluation phase, but also that this phase should emphasize the quality of the output of the model rather than merely the apparent quality of the model.

Does this really matter? Consider modeling the deforestation rate in the Amazon region of Brazil, as mentioned in the first chapter, and suppose that it is suggested that the model should be based on equating the supply and demand for wood. Doubtless a substantial model can be specified and estimated which on some criteria will seem to be satisfactory and to fit the data well. However if a decision maker decided to determine policy based on the model, attempting to control the rate of deforestation, it will almost certainly be unsuccessful because the model is based on an incorrect description of the basic driving forces. The major demand is not for wood but for the land on which the trees stand. If sufficiently careful methods of evaluation are used, the fact that the first model is unsatisfactory should become evident.

1 FOR Econometric models

The approach taken for the evaluation of models varies in different parts of the subject area. For example, cross-sectional and panel models are usually evaluated in-sample whereas time series models are also evaluated post-sample. To illustrate this difference, suppose one is interested in estimating the elasticity of demand for watermelons and has available some appropriate cross-sectional data set I. Two applied econometricians each build models, M_1 and M_2, using the same data and produce elasticity estimates $\hat{e}_1$, $\hat{e}_2$. If I am a decision maker wanting to use an elasticity value as an integral component of my decision, how do I decide which to use? If I ask a group of decision makers for advice, they are likely to expand a great deal of effort in comparing the quality of the alternative models. Values of summary statistics such as R^2, likelihood values and model selection criteria, for instance BIC, can be compared and even tested for superiority of one model over the other. Doubtless the properties of the estimation techniques used in deriving the models will be discovered and compared, including (asymptotic) consistency and relative efficiency. Potential problems with the alternative estimating methods will be emphasized.

It is possible to ask if M_1 encompasses M_2, or vice-versa, using alternative forms of encompassing. A single model can be viewed in terms of how well it performs under various "specification tests," against specific missing variables or linear trends or ARCH, general malaise such as non-linearity, the t-values of the included variables can be discussed, and the coefficients of variables queried as to their economic meaning as well as asking if their signs are "correct" according to some particular naive theory. However, all of this activity is aimed at discussing the (relative) quality of the models and ignores the quality of the outputs which I, as a decision maker, am most concerned about.

In contrast, consider a similar forecasting situation starting with a time series data set, two modelers produce models M_1 and M_2 and sets of one-step forecasts $f_{n+j,1}^{(1)}$, $f_{n+j,1}^{(2)}$ at (times) $n, n + 1, \ldots, n + N$, so $j = 0, \ldots, N$. Although it is standard practice to pay some attention to the relative quality of the models, the majority of the evaluation effort is directed to comparing the quality of the forecasts, that is to the outputs. As a decision maker having to choose between two methods of forecasting, it is the quality of the output that is more important rather than the quality of the model.

Why this difference of approach? There seems to be two obvious distinctions. The first is the idea that a decision maker will be using the output of the model for some previously stated purpose and that how well the models do in achieving this purpose provides a natural way of evaluating them. I think that decision makers appear more in discussion of time series evaluation than in those of cross-section or panel models. A second idea, which I think is now widely accepted by time series econometricians is that if M_1 produces better forecasts than M_2, it is unlikely that model M_2 will prove to be superior in other tasks such as testing theories or making control and policy statements.

The second explanation for the differences between the approaches is that, until recently, the cross-sectional analysis has been a "large-sample" form, with the number of parameters (q) in the models being very small compared to the sample size (n). Whereas in time series the potential number of parameters that can be used (number of variables times number of lags times number of equations = "curse of dimensionality") is large compared to the amount of data that are available. Although there are now a number of large time series data sets where this is not true, as discussed in Granger (1999), most important macroeconomic series are rather short, for example. This leads to worries that a model presented for consideration is the result of considerable specification searching (to use Leamer's (1978) term), data mining, or data snooping (in which data are used several times). Such a model might well appear to fit the data, in sample, rather well but will often not perform satisfactorily out-of-sample. It is the unfortunate experience with such overparameterized models that has led to the emphasis on post-sample evaluation in time series analysis. The experience is that the model that fits best in-sample does not necessarily forecast best. Examples using gold and silver prices can be found in Granger and Escribano (1998) and concerning simple neural networks and non-linear models in Granger and Teräsvirta (1992).

Although there is no equivalent to the "post-sample" in cross-section data, models can be evaluated using cross-validation techniques. This is where, say, 10 percent of the sample are randomly selected and dropped from the modeling procedure. The model so obtained is then evaluated in terms of its ability to fit the 10 percent that have been held back. The process can be repeated many times, excluding different groups and then averaged over cases. This method is found particularly helpful in time series modeling using parameter unparsimonious techniques such as neural networks. As always, it is easier to compare two models to find which is superior and sometimes to ask if combinations of the models are better than either, rather than trying to judge the quality of a single model. Models based on panel data sets are rarely evaluated by any modern techniques, although potentially they can use a mixture of cross-validation and true "post-sample" criteria. Examples are given in Granger and Huang (1997).

2 INF Evaluation of forecasts using squared costs

Early methods of evaluating forecasts ask, sensibly enough, how closely the forecast and the object being forecast resemble each other, but the measures used were not related to the decisions. Later, attention was centered on forecast errors e and then some rather arbitrary measures are used, such as the average absolute error or squared error to compare models. Tests of significance between these averages are not easily formed but alternatives are possible. An alternative approach to comparing a pair of forecasts is to form linear combinations of them and to see if the combination beats them both and which gets the higher weight. These methods represent the standard techniques for forecast evaluation. The concentration on errors can be justified as thinking of them as representing the costs arising from decisions that are imperfect because the forecast is imperfect, even though it might be optimal, given a particular set of information used in making the forecast. The idea is generalized in section 4.

2 FOR Evaluation of forecasts – the origins

If one initially considers one-step forecasts of x_{n+1} made at time n, denote the point forecast by $f_{n,1}$ or, for simplicity, f_n. The earliest attempts at evaluation, for example Theil (1966), considers the relationship between x_{n+1} and f_n, either graphically or by using OLS regressions, such as

$$x_{n+1} = \alpha + \beta f_n + \epsilon_{n+1}. \qquad (2.1)$$

The idea was simply that the better the forecasts the better the fit or relationship between these two series. Although sensible, this approach does not allow for the fact that the extent to which a series, such as x_{n+1} varies considerably across series. Granger and Newbold (1986) asked how these techniques worked when f_n was an optimal forecast, using a least squares criterion, and based on some "proper" information set $I_n:x_{n-j},\ w_{n-j}$. In this case it is found that in (2.1) one should get $\alpha = 0$, $\beta = 1$, and ϵ_{n+1} will be white noise. The result is easily generalized to the optimum h-step forecast, $f_{n,h}$, situation. We use the corresponding regression

$$x_{n+h} = \alpha + \beta f_{n,h} + \epsilon_{n+h} \tag{2.2}$$

which has $\alpha = 0$, $\beta = 1$, $\epsilon_{n+1} \sim MA(h-1)$.

These techniques assume that the cost function being used is least squares, so that if the forecast errors are defined by $e_{n,h} = x_{n+h} - f_{n,h}$ then the quantity being minimized is $E(e_{n,h}^2)$. The optimum one-step errors $e_{n,1}$ have the properties that $E[e_{n,1}] = 0$ and they are a white noise, so that $\text{corr}[e_{n,1}, e_{n+k,1}] = 0$ all $k \neq 0$. For h-step forecast errors $e_{n,h}$ similarly $E[e_{n,h}] = 0$ and they have the properties of an $MA(h-1)$ process, so that $\text{corr}(e_{n,h},\ e_{n+k,h}) = 0$, $k \geq h+1$. These properties are necessary but not sufficient that a set of forecast errors are errors from optimum forecasts.

When comparing a pair of sets of one-step forecasts, $f_{t,1}^{(1)}$, $f_{t,1}^{(2)}$ the natural criterion is to compare the two corresponding sums of squared errors

$$S_1 = \Sigma e_{1t}^2 \text{ and } S_2 = \Sigma e_{2t}^2 \tag{2.3}$$

when $e_{jt} = x_{t+1} - f_{t,1}^{(j)}$, $j = 1,2$. Applied studies often just present the post-sample values of these quantities but correct methodology would not let one just to prefer the smaller value but to test if one is significantly smaller than the other. The obvious test is an F-test, based on the ratio S_1/S_2, but the usual F-distribution does not apply as there are good reasons for expecting that e_{1t}, e_{2t} will be highly correlated, any surprise events that effect x_{t+1} will be likely to influence both e_{1t} and e_{2t}.

A simple method of testing the null hypothesis

$$H_o\colon E[e_1^2] = E[e_2^2] \tag{2.4}$$

was discussed in Granger and Newbold (1987, chapter 9) and later extended by Diebold and Mariano (1995). Let

$$d_t = e_{1t} - e_{2t}, \qquad s_t = e_{1t} + e_{2t}, \tag{2.5}$$

then H_o is equivalent to

$$H_o'\colon \operatorname{corr}(d_t, s_t) = 0$$

under various simple assumptions and any standard correlation test can be used, even a rank correlation test. If the null hypothesis is rejected, the smaller value of S_1, S_2 from (2.3) will indicate the superior forecasting method.

An entirely different approach is to consider the combination of forecasts using a regression approach

$$x_{t+1} = \alpha + \beta_1 f_{t,1}^{(1)} + \beta_2 f_{t,1}^{(2)} + \epsilon_{t+1}. \tag{2.6}$$

If $f^{(1)}$ dominates $f^{(2)}$ (or, equivalently, "forecasting encompasses") then β_2 will have an insignificant t-value, but β_1 will be significantly non-zero. Should domination not occur, then perhaps one is no longer interested in the question of which is the best of the two forecasting methods when a combination

$$c_{t,1} = \hat{\alpha} + \hat{\beta}_1 f_{t,1}^{(1)} + \hat{\beta}_2 f_{t,1}^{(2)} \qquad (2.7)$$

will be better than either, in terms of sums of squared errors. It is often possible to further improve the combination forecast by adding further terms such as x_t or lags of the various series to the regression.

3 INF Using general cost functions

Suppose that a decision maker decides that a forecast error of size e will result in a cost of $c(e)$, where the function c will increase as e increases in size, but not necessarily symmetrically, so that a positive error may not lead to the same cost as a negative error of the same magnitude. It can be taken that $c(e)$ will be positive except when the error is zero, when the cost is also zero. Optimal point forecasts, f, will be chosen to produce errors that, on the average, minimize this cost function. The properties of the errors that arise from generalized cost functions may be different from those that occur if the least-squares criterion is used, that is when $c(e) = e^2$. If the marginal cost is given by $c'(e)$, where c' is the derivation of the cost function, then using the errors from the optimum forecast, $c'(e)$ has mean zero, and so is unbiased, and also will have zero autocorrelations. These are usually the properties associated with errors from "rational expectations", but this is seen to be appropriate only if a least squares cost function is used. One can be "rational" and use a general cost function, and this can be tested by looking at the properties of the marginal costs, assuming that the cost function is known.

Consideration of general cost functions brings attention to what type of forecast information a model should provide. It has become common practice to provide just the expectation of the future value of the variable of interest, given the information being used, called the conditional mean. On some occasions, particularly in finance, the conditional variance is provided. For some cost functions these are enough to find the optimum point forecast, f, but in general, they are insufficient. In these latter cases, the whole predictive conditional distribution has to be specified.

3 FOR Evaluation using generalized cost functions

Suppose that there is a decision maker who takes a point forecast $f_{n,1}$ and uses it in some relevant decision. If the forecast is not perfect, so that $x_{n+1} \neq f_{n,1}$, which is typically the case, then a cost will arise because a sub-optimal decision will have been made. It will be assumed for the moment that the cost of this imperfect decision will be $c(e)$, where e is the forecast error, and $c(\ )$ is some cost function, having the properties

$$\left.\begin{array}{l} c(0) = 0 \\ c(e_1) \geq c(e_2) \text{ if } e_1 > e_2 > 0 \\ c(e_1) \geq c(e_2) \text{ if } e_1 < e_2 < 0 \end{array}\right\} \qquad (3.1)$$

so that $c(e)$ is monotonically non-decreasing as e moves away from zero. There is no reason why the cost function should be symmetric so that often $c(e)$ will have the property

$$c(e) \neq c(-e).$$

The obvious example is that the cost of being ten minutes early for a flight is quite different from being ten minutes late! This suggests that the least squares cost function $c(e) = ae^2$, with $a > 0$ will often be inappropriate for many decision makers.

Now suppose that we proceed under the assumption that the decision maker, who is the consumer of the forecasts having the properties of (3.1), has a known cost function $c(e)$. In practice this is not necessarily a very realistic assumption. Suppose that the producer of forecasts provides a prediction distribution $F_n(x) \equiv Prob(x_{n+1} \leq x | I_n)$ where I_n is some proper information set, and so includes $x_{n-j}, j \leq 0$. An optimal point forecast $f^o_{n,1}$ is obtained by

$$\min_{f_{n,1}} \int_{-\infty}^{\infty} c(x - f_{n,1}) dF_n(x). \qquad (3.2)$$

The corresponding forecast errors will be

$$e^o_{n,1} = x_{n+1} - f^o_{n,1}. \qquad (3.3)$$

It is shown in Granger (1999a) and elsewhere that these errors have the following properties:

$$\text{Define } z_t = c'(e^o_{t,1}), \qquad (3.4)$$

then

(i) $E[z_t] = 0$

(ii) $\text{corr}(z_t, z_{t-k}) = 0$, all $k \neq 0$,

so that z_t have the white noise properties.

(iii) in any regression

$$z_t = \alpha + \beta_1 z_{t-k} + \beta_2 g_{t-k}(I_t) + \text{error}, \qquad k > 0$$

where g is some component of I_t or function of such a component, then α and the β's are all expected to be zero. Note that if $c(e) = c^2$, the least square cost function, then $z = e$, so that z_t has all the familiar properties of e_t in this case. It should be noted that it is z_t which is unbiased in the general cost function case, not necessarily e_t. It may also be noted that most tests of whether a set of forecasts obey the theory of rational expectations do so within a least squares cost function framework. It is possible to be rational but to use a non-symmetrical cost function, for example. The test involving the regression between the actual and the forecast, in (2.1), is no longer necessarily relevant in this generalized cost function case.

Now consider what happens when we compare a pair of forecasting models M_1, M_2, which produce predictive distributions $F_n^{(1)}(x)$, $F_n^{(2)}$ respectively. A particular user will be assumed to have a cost function $c(e)$ and, using (3.2), will produce optimum forecasts denoted $f_{n,1}^{(1)}$, $f_{n,1}^{(2)}$ and corresponding errors

$$e_{n,1}^{(j)} = x_{n+1} - f_{n,1}^{(j)}, j = 1,2.$$

Given a set of these errors, the basic values to be compared are the average costs, which are proportional to

$$S_1 = \sum_n c\!\left(e_{n,1}^{(1)}\right), \ S_2 = \sum c\!\left(e_{n,1}^{(2)}\right),$$

the sums being over the available (post-sample) data set. As usual, it is difficult to test differences in value between S_1 and S_2 directly. However, it seems possible to use the sum and difference test as in (2.5) and later lines, but replacing e_{1t} by $[c(e_{1t})]^{\frac{1}{2}}$ and e_{2t} by $[c(e_{2t})]^{\frac{1}{2}}$, and then using a test of correlation.

The discussion is easily extended to h-step forecasting and to multi-step forecasting of differences of series, as in Granger (1999a). Combinations of forecasts can be considered by substituting for $f_{n,1}$ in (3.2) and the combination such as (2.7) and then finding $\hat{\alpha}$, $\hat{\beta}_1$, $\hat{\beta}_2$ to minimize the expected cost. I have no experience with this procedure.

Both Christoffersen and Diebold (1996) and Granger (1999a) consider a number of particular cost functions. It is easiest to condense the results in terms of what forecasts a forecaster may need to provide. Simple forecasts of the conditional mean

$$\mu_n = E[x_{n+1} \mid I_n]$$

and of the conditional variance $\sigma_n^2 = E[(x_{n+1} - \mu_n)^2 \mid I_n]$ have been traditionally considered enough, but more generally would be the provision of the predictive distribution $F_n(x) = \text{prob}(x_{n+1} \leq x \mid I_n)$. The sufficient forecasting requirement depends both on the form of the distribution of the process and the cost function. In the simplest case of all, if $c(e) = e^2$, then μ_n is the only forecast required, unless a forecast interval is also demanded, and then a new cost function will be needed for that. If the process has a location/scale form, so it can be written as

$$X_{n+1} = \mu_n + \sigma_n \epsilon_{n+1}$$

where ϵ_{n+1} is iid, and has distribution independent of I_n, then the optimum point forecast is

$$f_n = \mu_n + k\sigma_n$$

where k depends on the cost function. For the linex cost function

$$c(e) = \exp(\alpha e) - \alpha e - 1$$

one finds that $f_n = \mu_n + \alpha \sigma_n^2/2$. So again, knowledge of μ_n and σ_n is enough to obtain the optimum point forecast. However, these are exceptional cases; generally the integral minimization (3.2) has to be solved and so the full predictive distribution has to be supplied.

4 INF Users and cost functions

Although the previous sections suggested that ideally models should provide predictive distributions, in practice this rarely happens at this time. More usually, a model will provide just a point forecast and this produces a forecast error. Over time, a set of errors are generated from this first model. Suppose that there is a second model, which produces forecasts and thus a set of errors. To compare the two models if a user has a cost function $c(e)$, then the average costs, of the sets of errors, can be compared. We should expect that difficult users will have different cost functions, so that one user may find that the forecasts from the first model suit better, whereas another user will prefer the second model.

It is natural to ask if the forecasts from one model could be preferred to the forecasts from the other model for *all* users. This can be re-stated; is the distribution of errors from one of the models preferred to the other distribution of errors in terms of the expected value, for all possible cost functions. There is a concept from uncertainty theory, known as "second-order stochastic dominance" (or SOSD) which can be adapted for use with cost functions.

Second-order stochastic dominance is easier to contemplate if the two variables involved have the same mean. Then one distribution dominates the other, in the SOSD sense, if it is more compactly placed around the mean than the other distribution, remembering that any form of distribution can occur, not just Gaussian forms. To make this more precise, an integral inequality is required, as given in the formal section 4. The adaption to a somewhat different situation is called "Convex-loss stochastic dominance" (CLSD). It is used with cost functions which can be non-symmetric and thus do not have a one-to-one relationship with the utility function. A statistical test to compare the two distributions has yet to be devised for this adaptation, although a satisfactory one is available for second-order stochastic dominance.

If one distribution of errors is found to dominate another, and if it is plausible to expect sufficient stability in the situation, then this dominance should continue in the future and any new user can confidently use the better model regardless of the cost functions use.

4 FOR Different users have different cost functions

A fairly common feature of point-forecast evaluation is the observation that one method beats another using a least squares criterion, but that the ranking is reversed under some other criterion such as mean absolute errors. It is interesting to ask if it is possible for one forecasting method to generate forecasts that dominate those from a second method, under a wide variety of criteria. Suppose that the first method produces one-step forecasts $f_{n,1}^{(1)}$ with corresponding errors $e_{n,1}^{(1)} = x_{n+1} - f_{n,1}^{(1)}$, and similarly the second method produces forecasts and errors $f_{n,1}^{(2)}$, $e_{n,1}^{(2)}$. Suppose that the errors $e_{n,1}^{(1)}$ can be considered to come from a distribution $P_n^{(1)}(x)$, which can be well estimated from the accumulated histogram of past errors, and further suppose, for the time being, that it can be assumed the errors in the future will be drawn from this same distribution. Similarly, the errors from the second method will come from distribution $P_n^{(2)}(x)$. Further suppose, for convenience at this time, that $E[e^{(1)}] = E[e^{(2)}] = 0$. This assumption is relaxed later. One might expect that most users will prefer distributions which have probability density functions that are relatively bunched up around the mean compared to those that are less concentrated. From uncertainty theory the appropriate concept is called "second-order stochastic dominance" (with zero mean). The concept was introduced by Rothschild and Stiglitz (1980) and discussed and extended by Machina and Pratt (1997). For notational convenience we will now consider two variables: X with distribution function $F(x)$ and Y with d.f. $G(y)$. A condition for second-order stochastic dominance (with equal means), denoted $F >_2 G$ holds if and only if

$$\int_{-\infty}^{x} F(y)dy \leq \int_{-\infty}^{x} G(y)dy \text{ for all } x. \qquad (4.1)$$

If this occurs, an implication is that for any concave (strictly increasing) function $u(x)$ so that $u' > 0$, $u'' < 0$, then

$$E[u(X)] > E[u(Y)]$$

i.e.

$$\int_{-\infty}^{\infty} u(y)dF(y) > \int_{-\infty}^{\infty} u(y)dG(y). \qquad (4.2)$$

A utility function has these properties. Thus, this condition says that a decision maker will get higher expected utility if

F is used rather than G. A second implication is known as the "noise equation" which says that if $F >_2 G$ then Y and $X + \epsilon$ have the same distribution, written

$$Y \overset{d}{=} X + \epsilon \qquad (4.3)$$

where $E[\epsilon \mid X] = 0$ for all X. Although the statement here is that (4.1) implies (4.2) and (4.3), in fact each of these relationships implies the other two.

As suggested above, it is the traditional approach to think in terms of costs rather than utilities, but there is a basic difference. Whereas utilities are concave, cost functions have a minimum at $e = 0$, are convex, and need not be symmetric. In one particular case it is possible to immediately use second-order stochastic dominance theory, where the cost function is symmetric, so that $c(e) = c(-e)$. Now $c(e)$ can be considered to be just $c(|e|)$ and $|e|$ will take values on the positive line only. The previous theory, without the assumption of equal means, can be restated to give the result.

F will be said to second-order stochastically dominate G on the range $0 \le e \le M$, where M is some finite upper found if

$$\int_0^x [G(y) - F(y)] dy \ge 0 \text{ for all } x \text{ in } [0, M]. \qquad (4.4)$$

[The finite bound is a technical requirement and seems to have no practical consequences.] Implications are that

$$E[c(Y)] \ge E[c(X)]$$

$$\text{i.e.,} \int_0^M c(y)dG(y) \geq \int_0^M c(y)dF(y) \tag{4.5}$$

for *every* increasing function $c(\cdot)$ over $[0,M]$ so that $c'(e) > 0$, for all e in $[0,M]$. Further, the noise equation takes the form

$$Y \overset{d}{=} X + \epsilon \tag{4.6}$$

with $E[e \mid X] \geq 0$ for all X.

F second-order dominates G if any of the conditions (4.4), (4.5), or (4.6) holds as each implies the others, and each condition implies that the mean of F is less than or equal to the mean of G. It follows that if F second-order dominates G, then forecasting method 1 will be preferred by all users having a symmetric cost function.

In a paper to appear, Granger and Machina (1998) discuss a different form of stochastic dominance relevant for all cost functions, called convex-loss stochastic dominance (CLSD). F and G are a pair of cumulative distributions or $(-M,M)$ over the real line. They are CLSD if

$$\left. \begin{array}{ll} \int_{-M}^x [F(y) - G(y)]dy \leq 0 & \text{all } x \leq 0 \\[2mm] \text{and } \int_x^M [G(y) - F(y)]dy \leq 0 & \text{all } x \geq 0 \end{array} \right\}. \tag{4.7}$$

Implications are that $E[c(X)] \leq E[c(Y)]$; that is

$$\int_{-M}^M c(y)dF(y) \leq \int_{-M}^M c(y)dG(y) \tag{4.8}$$

for all convex $c(e)$ with a minimum at $e = 0$. The noise equation is now

$$Y \stackrel{d}{=} X + \epsilon$$

with sgn $E[\epsilon|X] \cdot$ sgn $(X) \geq 0$ so that for each X, $E[\epsilon|X]$ is zero or has the same sign as X. Further generalizations are possible but will not be discussed here.

The consequence of these results is that it is possible for one forecasting method to so dominate an alternative method in terms of the distributions of its one-step errors, that it is preferred by *all* users, regardless of their cost functions. By consideration of the noise equations it is possible to prove that if $f_n^{(1)}$, $f_n^{(2)}$ are the two sets of forecasts, then there is **no** combination of the form

$$c_n = \theta f_n^{(1)} + (1 - \theta) f_n^{(2)}$$

which dominates $f^{(1)}$, using each of the definitions of dominance. Although this is a restricted form of combination it is appropriate if both forecasts are optimum with respect to different information sets. This result links the dominance results with the idea of "forecast encompassing" described by Hendry (1995).

5 INF Origins of the forecasts

It is now appropriate to link the work in sections 3 and 4. If a user has a cost function $c(e)$, then point forecasts come from a process which produces errors that minimize the average cost. If there are two models and for any cost function optimum forecasts selected, errors produced, distributions of errors accumulated from experience, and if one model always dominates the other for every cost function, that model can be said to completely dominate the other. One model that will have this dominance property is the true data generating mechanism of the process being forecast, but if a model is found to completely dominate others, it is not necessarily the true data generating process.

5 FOR Where do the forecasts come from?

In the previous analysis one just started with a pair of forecasts and discussed properties of the errors, without any concern about how the forecasts were derived. Now consider the situation where the point forecasts are derived from predictive distributions using specific cost functions. For convenience suppose that the decision maker uses a cost function from a class of functions $c(e,\varphi)$. The point forecast $f_n(\varphi)$ is chosen by

$$\min_f \int c(\mathrm{x} - f_n(\varphi)) dP_n(x) \qquad (5.1)$$

and the subsequent errors are

$$e_n(\varphi) = x_{n+1} - f_n(\varphi)$$

and can be thought of as being drawn from a distribution with c.d.f. $F(x,\varphi)$ if the model is stationary.

If one starts with two alternative models M_1, M_2 which

produce predictive conditional distributions $P_n^{(1)}(x)$, $P_n^{(2)}(x)$, which then produces forecasts $f_n^{(1)}(\varphi)$, $f_n^{(2)}(\varphi)$ in conjunction with the cost function $c(e,\varphi)$, then corresponding errors will occur with marginal c.d.f.s $F(x,\varphi)$, $G(x,\varphi)$ respectively. It is reasonable to classify model M_1 as being superior to M_2 if

$$\int_{-\infty}^{\infty} c(x,\varphi)\,dF(x,\varphi) < \int_{-\infty}^{\infty} c(x,\varphi)\,dG(x,\varphi) \qquad (5.2)$$

for every φ. This is different than the condition (4.8) as the cost function and the distribution functions all depend on φ.

If one of the models, say M_1, is the true data-generating process for x_{t+1} then (5.2) will occur but it may be possible for (5.2) to occur without M_1 being the true d.g.p.

6 INF Comparing distributions

The previous discussion suggests that the consumers of forecasts, the users or decision makers, are generally better off if the producers of forecasts, the model makers, provide the whole predictive distribution of the future value of the variable of interest, given some specified information set, rather than just some summary statistics, such as a point forecast and a forecast of variance. How is a consumer to evaluate such a predictive distribution when provided? More practically, if there are a pair of alternative models available, each giving predictive distributions, which should be selected for decisions? A purely statistical criterion, such as using a comparison of likelihood values, often does not depend on the costs or benefits resulting from the decisions and so do not accord with the main thrust of the approach taken in this chapter.

Instead, a much more difficult but methodologically more satisfactory procedure is to associate a value with each combination of outcomes, that is the value that does occur of the variable being forecast, and of the decision, which will be assumed to depend on the whole predictive distribution, rather than just its summary statistics. The value can be considered as a benefit or a cost or possibly a utility, provided some method of actually measuring utility, rather than just ranking preferences, is available (at least for this discussion). For a model, these values can be considered as having been drawn from a distribution, a second model produces a second distribution of values, and a preference over the two models can be determined using second-order stochastic dominance.

6 FOR Comparing predictive distributions

It is clear from the previous discussion that users of forecasts are generally better off by being provided with $P_n(x)$ the whole predictive distribution of x_{t+1} given I_n, based on some model or empirical theory rather than some summary statistics, such as a conditional mean or a point forecast. The question that obviously arises is how to evaluate the quality of such a distribution. A natural measure is the log likelihood $L = \sum_n \log P'_n(x_{n+1})$ where $P'(x)$ is the probability density function corresponding to $P(x)$, assuming its existence, and n goes over some appropriate set of post-sample time values. As always it is easier to compare a pair of models, M_1 and M_2, to form their corresponding L values and to test if one is significantly better than another. West (1996) discusses how to form such a log-likelihood ratio test and White (1998) describes how a bootstrap technique can be used to obtain critical values for the test. However, these tests do not strictly relate to the idea of costs or values being faced by a decision maker when using forecasts.

To generalize earlier discussions, suppose that a decision maker bases the decision on the whole prediction distribution giving the decision made at time n $D(P_n)$ and that the "value" obtained from this decision, occurring at time $n + 1$, being a function of the decision and of the actual value taken by the series being forecast; i.e.

$$V(x_{n+1}, D(P_n)).$$

Value here can be considered as a "benefit," "cost," or "utility." Preference should be for some quantity that is strictly measurable. An example is given below. In a stationary situation, these values can be thought of as draws from a distribution with c.d.f. $F(x)$. If a different model produced decisions and thus values drawn from a distribution $G(x)$, one could compare these distributions using second-order stochastic dominance rather than just expected value. This approach generalizes those discussed earlier because decisions are based on the whole prediction distribution, rather than point forecasts, and are evaluated on the values generated jointly by outcomes and decisions rather than just from costs due to point forecast errors.

The procedure is, of course, much more difficult to undertake in practice but does give a methodological template that should be attempted in some form. Some practical aspects are briefly discussed in section 8. Although this discussion has been phrased in terms of the evaluation of forecasts, the underlying features are appropriate for the evaluation of any empirical model, even though a re-thinking of current standard practice is required. The basic emphasis is on the purpose of the model, the considerations of a decision maker, and thus a criterion for evaluation.

7 INF An example

To illustrate the ideas of the previous section, a very simple example is considered, with only two possible events, Good and Bad, and two decisions, Yes and No. For example, a Central Bank will contemplate inflation next month; if it is under 2½ percent, it will be Good, but over this percentage, will be Bad. Two decisions can be made, to raise core interest rates by ¼ percent, denoted Yes, or to leave them at their present level, denoted No. The decision will depend on forecast probabilities of the two events, which corresponds just to a forecast probability of Good, p_G and the probability of Bad, $p_B = 1 - p_G$. The pair p_G, p_B will comprise the whole predictive distribution in this case. These probabilities will depend on the model used and the information set and will thus change through time. For any decision maker, the choice of decision, Yes or No, will depend on these probabilities and on the values of the four combinations of event and decision that can occur. The bank can, it is assumed, put a value on the Good event occurring after the Yes decision and also on the Good event after the No decision, and so forth. Different bankers will have different values and so will not always agree on their decisions, even if the probability of a Good event is the same.

The analysis will depend on whether the decision maker is risk neutral, in which case decisions can be made on expected value, or risk adverse in which case stochastic dominance can be used to compare alternatives. A person is said to be risk neutral if there is no consideration of risk in his or her decisions. Obviously a risk adverse person is concerned about risk when making decisions, choosing less risky options when expected value is similar.

7 FOR A simple example

This example is taken from Granger and Pesaran (1998) where it is explored in more detail. It is a particularly simple case of the interaction of a decision maker and a forecaster. Its simplicity is useful because full details can be deduced and displayed. Suppose that a decision maker faces a situation in which there can be only two outcomes, denoted Good and Bad. The decision maker can either take an action

Table 3.1

		Event	
		Good	Bad
Decision	Yes	V_{GY}	V_{BY}
	No	V_{GN}	V_{BN}
Forecast probability		$p_{G,n}$	$p_{B,n}$

(denoted "Yes") or not take action (denoted "No"). For each combination of situations and decisions one can think of there being a corresponding value (or benefit or cost or utility – value will be used). Thus V_{GY} is the value that occurs if the Good event occurs and the Yes decision has been made (see table 3.1).

To help interpretation it is perhaps worthwhile considering a specific example. Suppose that the decision maker is a local city government considering whether or not to apply gravel and sand to the local roads on an evening when the roads might get icy overnight. A good event would be that the roads do not get icy; perhaps that the air temperature does *not* fall below $-2°C$, say, and a bad event is if the temperature does get at least this low. A "Yes" decision will be to apply sand to the roads, a "No" decision is not to apply sand.

On a standard good day with no sanding, the roads will have some value V_{GN} for the community. On a good day when the sand was applied unnecessarily, because of a wrong forecast, the value will be $V_{GY} = V_{GN}$ minus the cost of the sanding operation, so that $V_{GY} < V_{GN}$. If the roads are inflicted by icing, the sand will presumably be somewhat effective, so that one has

$$V_{BN} < V_{GN}$$
$$\text{and } V_{BN} < V_{BY}.$$

Suppose that at time n a forecaster produces a probability forecast $p_{G,n}$ that the good event will occur at time $n+1$, so that the probability that the bad event happens at n is $p_{B,n} = 1 - p_{G,n}$. Note that in this simple case the forecaster is providing the complete predictive distribution over all possible outcomes. The decision will have to be based on these probabilities. A likely form of the decision which will be assumed to hold here is that $D_Y \equiv$ Decision of "Yes" (take action) if $p_{B,n} \geq \theta$ so that $D_Y \equiv$ Decision of "No" if $p_{B,n} < \theta$, where, for the moment, θ is some undetermined constant. Below, $p_{B,n}$ will be replaced by just p_n for convenience.

At time $n+1$ the outcome event will occur, x_{n+1} in the usual notation, where here this variable can only take the forms of Good and Bad. We can write the following conditional probabilities:

$Q_{GY} =$ Probability (Outcome Good | Decision Yes)
$Q_{GN} =$ Probability (Outcome Good | Decision No)
$Q_{BY} =$ Probability (Outcome Bad | Decision Yes)
$Q_{BN} =$ Probability (Outcome Bad | Decision No)

Given a sufficiently long past history of forecasts and a stable situation, these probabilities can be estimated, assuming that all situations occur sufficiently often in practice.

If the decision maker is risk neutral, the expected values under the two types of decision can be compared

$$\left.\begin{aligned} EV_Y &= \text{Expected Value (Yes)} = V_{GY}Q_{GY} + V_{BY}Q_{BY} \\ \text{and } EV_N &= \text{Expected Value (No)} = V_{GN}Q_{GN} + V_{BN}Q_{BN} \end{aligned}\right\}. \quad (7.1)$$

For any particular forecast p_n and decision rule, here a value of θ, the "Yes" decision would be taken if $EV_Y > EV_N$ and the "No" decision if $EV_Y < EV_N$. Over the long run, the expected value received is

$$EV = EV_Y \, \text{Prob (Yes)} + EV_N \, \text{Prob (No)}. \quad (7.2)$$

The decision probabilities will depend on the properties of the forecast probabilities p_n and the value of θ, and so θ can be selected to maximize EV assuming that the distribution from which p_n is selected is stationary. In (7.1) it should be expected that θ will vary from one provider of forecasts to another. Two alternative forecasters would be judged in terms of the relative EV values they each achieve, the higher clearly being the better.

If the decision maker is risk averse, rather than risk neutral, for particular values of p_n and of θ, two discrete two-valued distributions have to be compared:

$$f_Y : V_{BY} \text{ (with prob } Q_{BY}\text{)}, \ V_{GY} \text{ (with prob } Q_{GY}\text{)}.$$

and

$$f_N : V_{BN} \text{ (with prob } Q_{BN}\text{)}, \ V_{GN} \text{ (with prob } Q_{GN}\text{)}.$$

From the inequalities established before, the locations of the probability points will be:

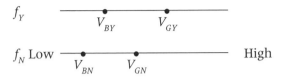

These points and their corresponding probabilities give the discrete distributions f_Y, f_N which can be compared using second-order stochastic dominance. If the Y distribution dominates the N distribution, the "Yes" decision should be made, and if N dominates Y, the "No" decision is appropriate. If there is no dominance, the decision can be made using expected values.

In the long-run, all four V values will occur with their associated Q probabilities. The resulting discrete distribution will depend on the decision rule, through the choice, and a value of θ, say $\theta°$, can be chosen so that the corresponding four point discrete distribution second-order stochastically dominates all distributions corresponding to other θ values, assuming that such a $\theta°$ exists and is unique.

Sets of probability forecasts $p_{n,1}$, $p_{n,2}$ from different models can be compared by applying dominance tests to the corresponding four point distributions, using $\theta_1°$, $\theta_2°$ as required.

If a forecaster provides a point forecast, rather than probability forecasts, of the good/bad events, say at time n forecasting "Good" if the forecast model produces a probability p_n which is less than some predetermined quantity φ, then the above analysis shows that this will produce a distribution that is dominated by the forecasts based on probabilities, provided $\varphi \neq \theta^\circ$. Since θ° will vary from one decision maker to another, depending on the relative size of the V values, it is seen immediately that point forecasts are generally inferior to probability forecasts.

8 INF Testing and estimating

The discussions above have been almost entirely theoretical. To be useful in practice, a variety of empirical questions have to be discussed. The two most important are how to test for second-order stochastic dominance, and other types of dominance, for one distribution over another; and how to produce predictive distributions, which may change with time. The formal section mentions a test for SOSD, which appears to be satisfactory, and various methods for producing predictive distributions, but these are insufficiently explored empirical research areas.

8 FOR Empirical implications

I will briefly discuss two practical implications of the above theory; how to test stochastic dominance and how to estimate predictive distributions. The first is not a well-developed area, for time series data, but Klecan, McFadden, and McFadden (1991) provide a useful robust test for second-order stochastic dominance. If $\hat{F}_1(x)$, $\hat{F}_2(x)$ are a pair of estimated cumulative distribution functions the test statistic used for the null of no second-order stochastic dominance is

$$T = \max_{x} \int_{-\infty}^{x} [\hat{F}_1(y)] - \hat{F}_2(y)]dy.$$

Critical values are found from a Monte Carlo procedure using a program made available in the above paper by Klecan *et al.* As a trial run we have used a set of six-month horizon forecasts and a corresponding set of three-month horizon forecasts and find that the latter set dominate, as expected. The test seems to be useable and reliable.

The question of how to provide a complete predictive distribution is an old one with many partial answers. If point forecasts of the mean, μ_n, and variance, σ_n^2, are provided by standard techniques, and if an assumption of normality is added, a whole distribution $N(\mu_n, \sigma_n^2)$, is derived. However, in practice the normality assumption is made rather causally and is not always properly tested. Alternative techniques can use forecasts of a variety of quantiles, e.g., Sin and Granger (1995) extended to multivariate situations by Chowduri (1996) and Kalman Filters using a mixture of normal distributions, due to Sorenson and Alspach (1971). The latter technique has been successfully used by control engineers for two decades and could be a useful starting point in economics.

An important question which needs further discussion is how to introduce time-varying parameters into predictive distributions, especially when parameters take large moves as in a structural break. Some progress in this area has been made by Clements and Hendry (1999) who generally consider just a pair of forecasts.

9 Evaluation of econometric models

It is now possible to continue the discussion that was initiated in the first section of this paper. To evaluate any empirical model it may not be enough to just discuss various statistical measures of the quality of a model or to compare one model to another, it is implausible to ignore the purposes of the model-building exercise, which is here taken to be to help a decision maker produce better decisions. The link between the model output and the resulting decision needs to be clarified as do the values associated with future outcomes of the process being studied and the decisions. Probabilities need to be associated with these values, either from observations or subjectively, producing a probability distribution of achieved values. Such distributions can be compared and possibly ranked using the techniques discussed above. I cannot contemplate a case in which a decision is evaluated without a passage of time, in which "future outcomes" are mentioned above. In practice, such a research program is very ambitious, and particularly as most economic model evaluation does not contemplate the relevance of users or their requirements. Once there is a change of attitudes, the possibility of following the suggested route will no longer seem so implausible.

The ideas expressed throughout this paper are by no means original, and are contained in work in the decision science areas; papers by Savage and others, and partly in meteorology. Although they have been with us for some time they have had little impact on practical empirical works and certainly deserve more attention.

References

Christoffersen, P.F. and F.X. Diebold (1996), "Further Results on Forecasting and Model Selection under Asymmetric Loss." *Journal of Applied Econometrics* 11, 561–572.

Clements, M.P. and D.F. Hendry (1999), *Forecasting Non-stationary Economic Time Series*. MIT Press: Cambridge, MA.

Diebold, F.X. and R. Mariano (1995), "Comparing Predictive Accuracy." *Journal of Business and Economic Statistics* 13, 253–265.

Granger, C.W.J. (1999), "Extraction of Information from Mega-Panels and High-Frequency Data." *Statistical Neerlandica* 52, 258–272.

    (1999a), "Outline of Forecast Theory using Generalized Cost Functions." To appear, *Spanish Review of Economics*.

Granger, C.W.J. and A. Escribano (1998), "Investigating the Relationship between Gold and Silver Prices." *Journal of Forecasting* 17, 81–107.

Granger, C.W.J. and L.-L. Huang (1997), "Evaluation of Panel Models, Some Suggestions from Time Series." UCSD Department of Economics Working Paper.

Granger, C.W.J. and P. Newbold (1986), *Forecasting Economic Time Series*. Second Edition, Academic Press: San Diego.

Granger, C.W.J. and M.H. Pesaran (1998), "A Decision Theoretic Approach to Forecast Evaluation." In preparation. First version, Department of Applied Economics, University of Cambridge Working Paper.

Granger, C.W.S. and T. Teräsvirta (1993), *Modelling Nonlinear Economic Relationships*. Oxford University Press.

Hendry, D.F. (1995), *Dynamic Econometrics*. Oxford University Press.

Klecan, L., R. McFadden, and D. McFadden (1991), "A Robust Test for Stochastic Dominance." MIT Working Paper.

Leamer, E.E. (1978), *Specification Searches*. Wiley & Sons: New York.

Machina, M. and C.W.J. Granger (1998), "Evaluation of Forecasts Using a Stochastic Dominance Approach." UCSD Department of Economics Working Paper.

Machina, M. and J.W. Pratt (1997), "Increasing Risk: Some Direct Constructions." *Journal of Risk and Uncertainty* 14, 103–127.

Rothschild, M. and J. Stiglitz (1970), "Increasing Risk: A Definition." *Journal of Economic Theory* 2, 225–243.

Sin, C.-Y. and C.W.J. Granger (1995), "Estimating and Forecasting Quantiles and Asymmetric Least Squares." UCSD Working Paper.

Sorensen, H.W. and D.L. Alspach (1971), "Recursive Bayesian Estimation using Gaussian Sums." *Automatica* 7, 465–479.

Theil, H. (1966), *Economic Forecasting and Policy*. North-Holland: Amsterdam.

West, K.D. (1996), "Asymptotic Inference about Prediction Ability." *Econometrica* 64, 1067–1084.

White, H. (1998), "A Reality Check for Data Snooping." Technical Report. NRDA, San Diego, CA.

Index

Index